Transforming Online Teaching in Higher Education

Transforming Online Teaching in Higher Education

Essential Practices for Engagement, Equity, and Inquiry

Steven Goss, Robin E. Hummel,
and Laura Zadoff

TEACHERS COLLEGE PRESS
TEACHERS COLLEGE | COLUMBIA UNIVERSITY
NEW YORK AND LONDON

Published by Teachers College Press,® 1234 Amsterdam Avenue, New York, NY 10027

Front cover art and design by adam bohannon design.

Library of Congress Cataloging-in-Publication Data is available at loc.gov

ISBN 978-0-8077-6864-8 (paper)
ISBN 978-0-8077-6865-5 (hardcover)
ISBN 978-0-8077-8187-6 (ebook)

Printed on acid-free paper
Manufactured in the United States of America

For Barbara Dubitsky—
Thanks for asking the right questions.

Contents

Transforming Online Teaching in Higher Education

Introduction

> The outcome of any serious research can only be to make two questions grow where only one grew before.
>
> —Thorstein Veblen, 1908

In this section we share pedagogical theories and knowledge that influenced our own practices for developing experiences that have fostered meaningful online learning for our students and ourselves.

SETTING THE STAGE

Online education is often presented as a disruptor to traditional higher education. One example that immediately comes to mind is how massive open online courses (MOOCs) provided access to content for millions of learners across the globe. This led students to question the cost of a college degree and inspired further discussions about the hierarchy of credentialing. Our focus, however, is on how the disruptive innovation of online education influences pedagogy. With new possibilities there is the opportunity to think about what we want our teaching to look like—to rethink our practices and to challenge the constraints of our physical classrooms. Four walls and a door are no longer essential for teaching and learning. In addition, connectivity is less of an issue, and access to the Internet is ubiquitous in institutions of higher education. Devices such as smartphones and tablets allow students to engage more easily and consistently with classmates and teachers; educational technologies continue to evolve with the ever-growing need for sophisticated digital resources. At some point the term *online education* will be antiquated, as education will no longer distinguish itself by the spaces (physical or virtual) where teaching and learning happen. In fact, we would argue that the obsolescence of this thinking has already begun, ushered in under the rapid adoption of online teaching and learning during the COVID-19 pandemic.

If you teach online, then being a disruptor may already resonate with you. Odds are, you enjoy the disruptive aspects of teaching online, even if you feel the need to talk about your practice in hushed tones, peppering your explanations with apologetic statements. Going online to teach is, in and of itself, disruptive. From the moment you make the decision to teach online, you are agreeing to reimagine your pedagogy. Case in point: When one of the authors of this book committed to teaching online, she had to reconstruct how she facilitated engagement. She accepted that she needed to try approaches that were unfamiliar to her while redefining what it meant for students to be present and engaged, and what presence and engagement meant for her as well. Going online means making a commitment to break free from familiar approaches to teaching and learning.

If teaching online provides opportunities for educators to disrupt their practice, then a progressive approach may also be attractive to those moving into online spaces. Progressive practice is often represented as a disruption to traditional teaching and learning. Traditional, in this sense, can be understood as using predetermined curricula intended to produce productive members of society. These efforts are often established by policymakers and authorized by administrators with little input from the teachers and students they impact. Conversely, the principles of progressive education promote highly personalized, active, and collaborative learning experiences with a focus on the learning community. It is these progressive principles that carry the potential to disrupt familiar practices.

To be clear, this book is not a manifesto for progressivism or for online education. Instead, it is a resource for strengthening our understanding of what we believe are the affordances of online teaching and learning. We will examine how the practices of progressive educators can be useful for teachers new to the online classroom and for experienced online educators seeking to enhance their existing practices. Going online encourages teachers to think about the true meaning of engagement: One can no longer fall back on the presumption that learning is happening simply because we are sharing a physical space with our students. Does anyone truly believe that students are learning simply because they are sitting in front of us, nodding their heads like cooperative receptacles of our insightful wisdom? If only.

OVERVIEW OF CHAPTERS

Kohn (2015) wrote that it is fitting that progressive education does not have a fixed definition because of its "reputation for resisting conformity and standardization" (p. 2). He pointed out that progressive educators differ on the meaning of a progressive approach:

> Some people focus on the unique needs of individual students, while others invoke the importance of a community of learners; some describe learning as a process, more journey than destination, while others believe that tasks should result in authentic products that can be shared. (p. 2)

However, Kohn argued that there is enough of an understanding to agree on a set of values that embody progressive education. He defined these values as attending to the whole learner, community, collaboration, social justice, intrinsic motivation, deep understanding, active learning, and taking the learner seriously (2015, p. 2). The concepts informing each chapter of this book—engagement, inquiry, equity, presence, community, and time and space—serve as lights to illuminate compelling practices for online education. These concepts, aligned with the values Kohn has shared, influence our development of meaningful online practice.

There are six main concepts that we will focus on as interrelated building blocks for developing an enriched and enlightened online experience. We will be sharing different strategies for implementing these concepts and inviting others to share how these concepts have influenced their online practice. Chapter 1, "Engagement," explores how we invite learners to be involved in the discussions and activities of an online course. We define engagement as an interaction measured not in magnitude, but by the way the learners encourage one another to contribute to a sustained, thoughtful, and purposeful discussion. Chapter 2, "Inquiry," explores the online classroom as a space where experiences are informed by student questions, interests, and curiosities. Teachers can adapt their lessons, activities, and assignments to respond to and expand the inquiry of the learning community. Chapter 3, "Equity," explores how equity is essential to online learning and argues for the importance of building an environment where all voices are heard, students have the opportunity to lead and guide discussions, and all learners support one another in ways that serve to strengthen learning and provide access to knowledge. Chapter 4, "Presence," explores how teachers and students construct worthwhile learning experiences by developing a social, cognitive, and teaching presence (Garrison et al., 1999). Learners are encouraged to form meaningful connections by contributing to and sustaining discourse. The teacher facilitates these connections and discussions by interacting with the students through reflection, synthesis, and feedback. Chapter 5, "Communities," explores the potential of the online classroom as a learning community where all learners contribute to inquiry, knowledge, and expertise. These contributions inform and deepen the understanding of what is taught in the course. The digital space also provides a unique opportunity for learners to be a part of other communities and share what they are learning in those communities with their classmates. Chapter 6, "Time and Space," explores the digital classroom as an opportunity to collaborate and communicate outside a defined meeting time and place. This unconstrained structure enables students to move through the course experience at a pace aligned with how they learn, providing teachers and students more time for reflection and synthesis. This open and flexible structure offers students a more sustained and ongoing experience, giving them agency in the course that benefits them as learners. The book ends with Chapter 7,

"Conclusions: Shifting Your Mindset and Sifting Through Your Residue," which suggests signposts and pathways for new and experienced educators to grow their online practice. We consider how the different concepts described in Chapters 1 through 6 are connected to an evolving pedagogy and conclude by examining lingering issues and encouraging readers to expand the possibilities for teaching and learning online.

Inside this book you will also encounter quotations from the people we interviewed that enrich the narrative and give you additional food for thought. We had so many long and thoughtful conversations with seasoned and inventive online educators, who all made wonderful points on teaching and learning that added to the scope of ideas we had for the book. Throughout each chapter you will find breakout boxes and bars that highlight quotes from our interviews that were provocative and inspired our online practices. We have split the breakouts into four categories: *For Your Consideration*, *Counterpoints*, *Quotables*, and *Tips*.

- *For Your Consideration* includes quotes to make you think. They may be grounded in established educational theories or the interviewee's own personal philosophies for online education.
- *Counterpoints* are quotes that may make you question your own assumptions. These are quotes that counter the narrative we have written.
- *Quotables* are interesting statements or thoughts that we could not leave on the cutting room floor. They are there to drive home the points in the chapters.
- *Tips* are quotes that are the closest thing to a how-to you will find in this book. They are strategies that teachers use for online teaching and learning.

Each chapter closes with some questions for you to ponder. We have based these on the questions that the chapters raised for us as we read through the interviews and wrote our thoughts on what we discovered. These questions are offered so that you may take a moment to pause and consider what you have read and reflect on how the concepts influence your thoughts on what teaching and learning look like in the online environment.

As you read this book, keep in mind that this is not a manual for teaching online. It is meant to be a spark, a seed, a worthwhile contribution to your online practice. We invite you to think more deeply about how to teach learners in digital spaces. How do you think about learners as pacesetters, inquirers, and community members? How do you think about spaces as flexible, fluid, and continuous? It is our hope that by sharing these concepts we broaden your understanding of what is possible for teaching and learning in a rapidly changing world.

OUR THEORETICAL FRAMEWORK

We define progressive education as "the act of teaching [and learning] that derives from reflection and which inspires reflection again" (Stommel et al., 2020, p. 4). We proceed from the progressive belief that powerful teaching is grounded in inquiry and community, taking into account the world educators live in, the students they teach, and the tools they use to bring teaching and learning to life (Dewey, 1938). We will use this approach to demonstrate that moving teaching and learning online is an opportunity to redesign how one teaches and to use that design to further reflect on how one can strengthen practices for the online classroom.

Critical Pedagogy

Critical pedagogy (Freire, 1993; Giroux, 2011) connects teaching and learning by supporting all learners in the continuous process of inquiry and reflection, and in seeing the connection between knowledge and power. Critical pedagogy supports the learner's stance by supporting the development of voice and power. Taking a critical pedagogical approach focuses the intellectual content of teaching on inquiry, reflection, relationships, and research.

In a progressive teaching experience, students and teachers are expected to think critically about their own learning and its relationship to the content being taught (Cochran-Smith & Lytle, 2001). A critical pedagogical framework requires us to take an independent and critical learner's stance in order to challenge the perspective that online teaching is not as good as teaching on ground. An educator who has critical pedagogy as a theoretical framework on-ground will embrace a progressive stance online. Supporting all learners to think critically about their own learning and their relationship to coursework gives teachers and their students the power to take ownership of the course and stand steadfast against an authoritarian system that maintains that students are empty pails waiting to be filled (Freire, 1993). Furthermore, in building one's online teaching practice, it is imperative that faculty challenge the hegemonic presumption that they are the only experts in the room. Resisting this presumption makes it possible for students to develop the critical consciousness necessary for being active participants in their own learning (Brookfield, 2000).

Faculty examine their work as an intellectual endeavor in order to illuminate the essential idea that to be a teacher means to be a learner. Knowledge as something bestowed on those who do not know by those who are assumed to know negates knowledge as a process of inquiry among learners. Teachers are not delivery systems and their students are not passive receptacles. Knowledge does not move in a one-way, linear direction. When knowledge comes through a one-way discourse, learners do not need to interact with each other or with the material. Critical pedagogy requires the learner to take an activist's role and have a purposeful voice in their experiences of learning. Shor and Freire (1987) explained that the process of learning is a dialectical one; teachers are in a mutual learning relationship with students. This is how critical pedagogy can become the paradigm for a more nonhierarchical approach to online teaching and learning. A critical pedagogical framework supports an approach to online learning that diminishes the hierarchy by which many students feel disenfranchised and creates a community that is essential for a sound online course.

Appreciative Inquiry

Appreciative Inquiry (Cooperrider & Whitney, 2005) promotes a supportive and collaborative inquiry that is essential to a progressive approach for learning online. The appreciative aspect focuses on the positive core of our work and what inspires us. Appreciative Inquiry promotes ownership of craft, champions one's voice, and engages learners in seeing their work as an intellectual endeavor.

We would argue that any vision of teaching that does not articulate how one's practice relates to hope for the future is a purposeless vision. We begin with Appreciative Inquiry by respecting the energy with which teachers are trying things out online and embracing ways in which teaching online has informed their practice. Buoyed by the focus on topics that are important to us personally, we create our work in a way that would inspire us to be scholar-practitioners and not merely competent transmitters of knowledge.

Those of us who study online teaching move beyond theory and develop a sense of what new questions we must ask ourselves in order to move this intellectual endeavor forward. Appreciative Inquiry is helpful in embracing the challenge of listening deeply and respectfully in a way that nurtures relationships. Unlike a technical approach to owning our practice or a list of things to master in order to effect change, Appreciative Inquiry is a thought process that focuses on identifying what works and analyzing how to do more of what works (Hammond, 2013).

The emphasis on appreciation comes from the idea of the appreciative eye in art (Carr-Stewart & Walker, 2003). As teachers deepen their craft through teaching online, they learn to collaborate with an open heart and mind, and to be vulnerable and open in their work with colleagues. At its essence, Appreciative Inquiry involves "the art and practice of asking questions that strengthen a system's capacity to apprehend, anticipate and heighten positive potential" (Carr-Stewart & Walker, 2003, p. 10). At its essence, teaching online involves the art and practice of asking questions that strengthen our capacity to own and deepen our work. Carr-Stewart and Walker (2003) explained that in Appreciative Inquiry, people accept the paradoxes of a system, accept that change is an iterative and sometimes slow process, embrace the idea that there are many ways to approach change, and understand that in order to effect change we need to attend to our relationships. Appreciative Inquiry entails focusing on what works in our teaching and building on it.

WHY WE WROTE THIS BOOK

Why did we decide to write a book on online teaching and learning? Because going online inspired us to examine our pedagogy more closely and we wanted to share that experience with others. This is the story of our online teaching experiences and the stories of friends and colleagues who encouraged us to transform our practices. As John Seely Brown (2002) said, "Learning is a remarkably social process" (p. 65). In an effort to pursue the progressive practice we promote, we did not write this book alone. This work provided a wonderful opportunity to learn from others who also made a conscious, and possibly daring, leap into the digital ether to teach. This has been an occasion to make explicit what we have learned, and to tap into an existing knowledge ecology made up of students, faculty, researchers, instructional designers, edtech professionals, and anyone else who has courageously entered into a digital classroom.

We interviewed practitioners who we knew were teaching online and had great stories to tell about their experiences. Interviews were held via videoconference, and while the focus of the interviews varied depending on who we were interviewing, we always asked them to describe their online teaching experience and specifically asked about a practice they cherished. We interviewed 37 practitioners, all of whom teach undergraduate and graduate students in different disciplines. Most of them had been teaching online before 2020, but some taught entirely online for the first time during the pandemic.

We conclude our introduction by contributing three watershed moments from our practice to the evolving knowledge ecology. These vignettes illustrate points of inspiration from our own journeys. We hope these anecdotes will set the stage for the rest of the book: When did we observe that what we were doing significantly contributed to the growth of our online teaching practice?

Steve's Vignette

A student of mine mentioned that even though she had "felt least successful" in my online course, she had also "learned the most." I was not sure how I should think about that at first, but it became clear that an affordance of teaching online is that there are many ways for students to review, revisit, and assess the knowledge being fostered and the work being shared. Students can actively reflect on and contribute to ideas and create their own measures of success based on their engagement in the learning community. My student "learned the most" because of her high level of interaction, and yet felt her own final project, which was thoughtful and well done, might have been stronger based on what she was experiencing in the course environment. This demonstrated how online learning is more than a static collection of information. Learning online produces an evolving body of knowledge that students can review, revisit, collect, curate, and dig through to add to their own comprehension throughout the course. So she values that she has "learned the most" because she came to measure success not simply by the final project's grade or quality, but over a holistic learning experience. When students can spend more time following ideas that interest them and engage in experiences where knowledge is gathered rather than content delivered, the learning for the entire community is enhanced. This was an important turning point for me.

Robin's Vignette

There was a watershed moment early in my online teaching experience when I recognized the affordances that online learning offers. I was teaching a new online leadership course called "Technology and School Change." The topic of teaching handwriting in the early elementary grades came up parallel to a topic I had explicitly assigned. As the students attended to the perfunctory requirements of my forum assignment (like the dutiful students they were), they also began another thread, engaging in the controversy around teaching handwriting in early elementary education. They posted links to articles that offered various arguments and the exchange they had was heated, substantive, and enlightening. It went on *for over two weeks*, with references continuing to emerge throughout the course. While students attended to all the required assignments, most of them did not generate as much energy as the handwriting topic. In addition, this discourse did not stop when the lesson changed. This is why I love teaching online: The ongoing engagement supports me as a learner. I discovered that I didn't always have to be the facilitator of the learning and that learning continued beyond and actually transcended my facilitation and direction. In an online environment, it is easier not to be the center of attention. I am one more voice and I don't have to worry that my role as the teacher hijacks the conversation.

Laura's Vignette

An informative experience I had was designing and facilitating an introductory course called "Faculty Blended Course for Blended Teaching and Learning." This course provided faculty with an opportunity to discuss and integrate online experiences into their teaching. In selecting which formats I used for the course (in-person, synchronous, or asynchronous), the questions behind my decisions—What is best for students? What is best for the content of the course? What are the teachers' strengths and desires for the course?—were essential issues to consider. One example of this decision-making was my original plan for our first session. I thought it had to be in person; however, I found out that some faculty would not be able to attend on site. This challenged my thinking. I felt strongly that the first session of a blended course should be in person to set the tone for discourse and community. But I also felt strongly that everyone should be present for this session. So I moved it online. In making this decision, flexibility and inclusivity took precedence over the format. While I had criteria for making decisions based on aspects I value from each format, ultimately, the decisions I made ended up achieving the collaborative experience I wanted teachers to have. This experience should provide assurance to teachers that they too will make sense of their online practice, even if it challenges their existing beliefs.

These vignettes demonstrate how teaching online made aspects of our practice that were previously unknown to us, known. We now understand how online teaching has the potential for:

- Students to see their courses as documents of their thinking and the thinking of others, and to use that documentation to reflect on their learning;
- Teachers to deepen their understanding of their teaching presence and how that presence supports equity of voice;
- Teachers to adapt the flexibility of blended formats for shaping access and community.

We believe it would be capricious for us to ignore the power that online teaching and learning has had in advancing our practice. Sharing these stories has helped us to think about what the future of teaching and learning can be. Of course, these stories can be received as empowering or detrimental. And yes, for every utopian view there is a dystopian response. However, we want to encourage you, dear reader, to go forth with the optimism we have. Our experiences have inspired us to continue to teach online, even when it was frowned upon. These experiences inspired us to deepen our practices when we wanted to rest on our laurels. We hope that by the end of this book, you will be equally inspired. We hope that through your willingness to join us on this journey to explore online teaching and learning, something that was unknown to you before will become known, and you will be inspired to share an affirming story of your own.

CHAPTER 1

Engagement

> So much of what's done badly in an online course comes from the disingenuous ways we create engagement. My advice to faculty is that you can create 11 great lectures that don't matter. Students can also read a book with 11 great chapters. We're not creating just the content, we're creating a classroom experience. If it's just about reading your lecture or your curated reading list, then that's not a class.
>
> —Kristine Rodriguez Kerr

This chapter explores how we invite learners to be involved in the discussions and activities of an online course. We define engagement as an interaction that cannot be measured in magnitude, but by the way the learners encourage one another to contribute to a sustained, thoughtful, and purposeful discussion.

DISTINGUISHING BETWEEN PARTICIPATION AND ENGAGEMENT

Our exploration of the building blocks that make for an enriched and enlightened online practice begins with engagement. We thought it was appropriate to start here because we find that teachers new to online teaching are particularly concerned with understanding engagement and what it looks like online. With each concept we introduce, the question of how that concept looks will be the implicit foundation for the practices being presented, illustrating how these concepts can embolden the learning experience online. When seeking to understand the experience of an online class, engagement can be a good jumping-off point because all teachers tend to have a working definition for what classroom engagement is. The challenge educators have when entering into the online space is that the definitions and measures they use for engagement often depend on student interactions in physical spaces.

The example that often comes up when teachers think about classroom engagement is that of the students sitting at their desks, raising their hands, or maybe getting together in a circle to share their thoughts on the topic at hand and to receive feedback from the teacher. Engagement between the teacher and the student is corporeal; we see our students, we hear them, we sense them as bodies taking up space. And yet understanding student engagement in the material classroom is challenging. How does a teacher know that the thoughts and actions of every student in the classroom are truly on task? If the engagement between the students and teachers actually sitting together is uncertain, then engagement in the online classroom can only be even more so. How does one develop and assess engagement in spaces where the learning experience is distant and mediated?

The challenge to understanding engagement in digital spaces is the same as understanding it in the in-person classroom. How does one distinguish between the student who is engaged in a learning moment and one who is simply present? Or between a student who is actively working to inspire discussion and one who is just responding to a request made by the teacher? To go beyond this perfunctory level of participation is to play a part in the class by contributing informed and thoughtful responses to discussions, sharing meaningful and pointed ideas, presenting conscientious project work, asking inspired questions, adding commentary to the content and concepts being explored, and advancing the inquiry being fermented by the general activity of everyone involved in the learning experience.

This activity of the mind does not depend on physical presence. However, as instructors, we have been primed to recognize student engagement through the student's physical representation of their mental activity, or at least the physical actions that we have come to believe signify engagement. There are certainly moments in the in-person classroom where the student's physical response equates to the demonstration of struggle and ideation and the teacher is witness to the birth of a new skill or understanding. But learning in an online environment does not allow for a visceral reaction to students' emotive and kinetic responses. Students learning online do so outside of traditional time-based structures and are able to take their time. Their mental actions and responses take priority. They are able to draft ideas and understanding. They can read, reflect, and read again what others have shared, posting when they feel they have truly grasped the ideas being explored and the concepts being taught. But even if you agree that the active mind can represent itself

For Your Consideration

Your job as a teacher is to get the students as excited about something as you are. How do you get them to see why this content excites you? Share your story with them. I think when you can get the student excited about something, that's when learning can happen. When they connect with it. When they see some sort of passion for it, or some sort of use for it. —Julie Coltharp in digital spaces, you may still find yourself asking, "Yes, but what does that representation look like?"

Asking what engagement looks like online is a fair question, but it shouldn't be asked in an effort to understand its distinction from engagement in the physical classroom. Good student engagement in any learning space goes beyond physical presence and mere participation. In seeking to understand student engagement online, we shouldn't start by making comparisons between the physical space and the digital space; instead, we should start by considering what makes any learning engaging, whether it is in person or at a distance, and asking what stifles student engagement and how those obstacles can be avoided in any environment where learning is situated.

DESCRIBING THE ENGAGED ONLINE CLASSROOM

In an engaged learning environment, students are encouraged to examine the learning they are involved in, adding new discoveries and knowledge to the conversations being developed throughout the course. In order for a classroom to be engaged, students need to be involved in the shaping of the discourse. Students must also be challenged by, and challenge, what is being taught. Dave Cormier, a digital learning specialist in the Office of Open Learning, University of Windsor (Ontario, Canada), described a classroom that lacks engagement as a classroom where "the process of learning is really just the process of obedience." Students may appear to be engaged, but that engagement, as Cormier described, is just "a weird gifting game" where the teacher says, "'I give you a ball and you give me back the ball,' and the student responds, 'I've been told, I have given you back what you gave to me.'" This act of the student receiving information from the teacher and then giving that information back to the teacher, Cormier says, "makes everybody feel like they've engaged in something." Cormier helps to clarify that if engagement is to be authentic within the context of learning, the teacher must shift to more of a guiding role, such as that of a course developer, learning mentor, or expert advisor. The teacher should act as a member of the learning community they are constructing, not its sole architect. An experience where the students are as responsible for their learning as the teacher is a good basis for understanding the development of an engaged online classroom. The classroom should be a space where the teacher encourages students to seek out resources beyond those that the teacher alone can provide. Teachers should embrace the opportunities that learning online affords, where students may locate other sources of information on the course subject and find information and analysis unknown to the teacher. This may be a challenging concept, especially if most of your teaching has taken place in physical classrooms. As Cormier explained, "In an environment where students are guiding things, you have to be comfortable with uncertainty. And I think for a lot of faculty, the reason why they overstructure their online courses is that they're not sure they're going to be able to handle the uncertainty coming back from their students." And yet it is this same uncertainty that can encourage engagement to thrive in online environments. Cormier added,

> The fantasy of the cone of scarcity that we create in a face-to-face classroom is not possible to enact online. What we've managed to do in the last 20 years is create this cone of scarcity inside the university classroom, where we say turn off your computers and don't use your phone. And so a teacher can maintain the idea that they are the fount of knowledge inside the classroom. And yet online students are not bereft of that power. If I say, "This is true." and a student finds an equivalent expert who says the opposite, online, there's no way for a teacher to close that off.

This is how engagement in the online classroom starts to take shape. As we understand student engagement inside the microcosm of the walled classroom as an active and authentic engagement among everyone there, we can see how the online classroom extends that by encouraging students to expand on who they consider a go-to resource for information and knowledge. The teacher can set foundations and then step away from the center, encouraging the students to engage with peers and external experts who now become a part of the learning community. And that brings us back to the question, What does engagement look like in the online classroom? The common lecture-based model in which the teacher presents the student information and asks for that information back does not translate well online (if we can even say it worked well on site). Instead, online educators see themselves as the inspiration for divergent learning experiences that branch off from the teacher to the students, the students to their peers, and the class to the world at large.

Clay Shirky, a longtime thinker and writer about the Internet who is presently associate professor and vice provost at New York University, affirmed that the online classroom, and quite possibly any classroom, is a collection of experiences, emerging from everyone who is involved with the intent of connecting collectively to learn about and from each other. He explained, "What you get for free when you gather a group of people in a classroom is a kind of sense of each other." When developing an online course, teachers should consider, first and foremost, how to establish the learning space as a space for the encouragement of student congregation and interaction. This does not imply that the teacher must develop a series of prompts and open forums designated for assigned engagement. Instead, the teacher should consider how to provide opportunities and spaces that are open to students sharing and conversing, coming together to know each other as learners. As Shirky described, although these experiences can be created by faculty, if the space is open and flexible, experiences that encourage engagement may also develop out of interactions among the students. If the driving goal is to encourage engagement, then these types of engaged experiences can, as Shirky noted, "unfold in many ways." While the teacher may develop the foundational activities and actions to spark interaction, the online classroom should be adjustable, allowing for all involved to create opportunities for engagement. We can think of our online courses and ask: What are the different ways that these experiences can unfold? Before we can answer, we must be open to seeing online learning as distinct from the classrooms moored to the lecture-based models of student–teacher back-and-forth Cormier described. In developing an online course, the approach one should start with is that the classroom is a space for engagement and activity and not for lecturing and testing. If you are able to do this, then it is that much easier to turn the smallest activities into rich engagements, which in turn go a long way toward an engaged online experience. Take, for example, a small activity that Shirky shared. Ten minutes before the start of the synchronous course he teaches, he opens the video conference for the students. He explained that he does this so that if anyone comes in, they can connect with each other, giving him the opportunity to observe the students vocalizing their ideas prior to the class discussion and immediately establishing the voice of the student as a part of the learning community. Shirky explained that if he does not bring student voice into the experience from the beginning, the students "drop back into 'watching TV' mode rather than 'I'm in conversation with people' mode."

Classroom discussion is crucial to student engagement. Whether that discussion is activated by the teacher, the students, or an external member of the learning community, the conversations that occur within the classroom are essential to establishing a sense of engagement and making certain students are not defaulting to TV-watching mode, or if the course is asynchronous, mailing-it-in mode. In an asynchronous course, the discussion forum is a critical component. In fact, we suspect that if you asked a colleague to describe what they thought an online course looked like, they would describe the discussion forum as the online course. Most who have taught online will have experienced a moment where they found dissatisfaction with the forums, often stating that they want something more without really knowing what they are missing. This frustration is

COUNTERPOINTS

God bless Quality Matters [rubric for assessing online learning quality] for providing a checklist, right? Because there's a bunch of stuff that you can mess up. Checklists are good for, "Don't make these mistakes." They keep you from going into the ditch, but they don't have to keep you from moving forward." —Clay Shirky usually attributed to the dull "post a response and reply to someone else" expectation that is common of many online forums. The teacher posts a prompt, and the students post their answers, and not much else happens. This type of perfunctory participation does not produce a strong sense of engagement and leaves the teacher longing for the more unconstrained experience that an in-person discussion can generate.

However, in an online course, the forum is where engagement can really take off, and accepting the forum as a primary space for student interaction can help teachers to better understand engagement in the online environment. The challenge is to come to the discussion forum with an open mind. Kristine Rodriguez Kerr, academic director and clinical associate professor for the MS in professional writing at the NYU School of Professional Studies, explained:

> The way I think about a good face-to-face course is that it's not a big lecture with one person talking. It's about the conversation that happens across faculty members and students. And that's what I'm trying to recreate in the forum space. The forum is where you have your interaction point. You are teaching with prompts that are really interrogating where the students are. Who are they in relation to the content? And so that's the practice that I'm trying to capture; the magic that happens in a classroom that's about engaging in a sustained way with a group of students guided by a faculty member over a semester. That's what we have to try to recreate and that's what I've come to because of online teaching. It's really helped me understand that an online course isn't a website. It isn't a book. It isn't curated lectures. It's not a TED talk. It's about getting groups into conversations in meaningful and thoughtful ways and inviting people in with the teacher participating as much as they're participating. This is what makes an online class.

An asynchronous classroom is not a digital textbook to be read alone, but an abundance of provocative activities and prompts inspired by the real-time responses from student discussions that encourage students to share their thoughts and questions with one another. Similarly, a synchronous classroom is not a passive screen experience, but an opportunity to connect diverse voices across different spaces. Online courses are not passive experiences. Students should be actively driving the learning that is occurring in the classroom.

The tools that the majority of learning management systems (LMS) use for communication and collaboration provide teachers and students with the bare necessities. Forums, for example, are not designed to be engaging, but to support communication where one person speaks, and then the next person, and so on. So engagement online does not lie with the tools that are meant to support discussion, interaction, and collaboration, and that's fine, because engagement was never about the desks or the chalkboard either.

Instead, it is about the ways in which the teacher inspires and supports student communication and collaboration. The more we accept that the tools used for online teaching and learning exist as a tabula rasa, a space where teachers and students can design and develop all kinds of activities and experiences to bring students together for learning, the more we can look beyond the tools to see what online engagement looks like and how we achieve it.

CREATING ENGAGED CLASSROOM EXPERIENCES

For influential writer and thinker Howard Rheingold, engagement is, simply put, "giving the students active things to do." And while he may be using shared whiteboards, chat boards, and, as he describes it, a "Wikipedia style," it is the activities that he develops for those various tools, both within the LMS and outside of it, that work to engage the students in his classroom. His approach to making the online classroom active is to establish an assortment of roles for students to support the learning experience. As he described, "We put up a whiteboard, brainstorm different roles, and then learners sign up for different roles. So one role that two or three people could take during a session was 'searchers.'" Rheingold explained that the searchers would explore the web for references appropriate to the discussions taking place in the classroom, posting a URL to any reference in the class chat. Then another group of students would take those URLs and act as "bloggers," writing a three-sentence description as to why students may want to review the reference provided. From there the roles expanded based on the needs identified by the class. There was a group who would do mind mapping. Another group would act as lexicographers, who identified words and phrases that appeared in the readings, lectures, and online discussions. They developed their own resources to collect the output of the different roles they adopted. As he described it, "We had a wiki page and it was the job of everybody to fill out the lexicon, adding definitions and alphabetizing links. And with a wiki you can tell who did what and at the beginning of each class I could show the students who did what. All of the learners would be responsible for transferring their material to a 'wiki master,' who would then create a wiki page for the material they had collected." These roles as searchers, bloggers, contextualizers, lexicographers, and mind map developers provided the students opportunities to engage in the learning and with each other.

> **Quotables**
>
> There are more similarities than differences between good online teaching and good teaching. And that's what we have to remember.
> —Kristine Rodriguez Kerr

Tools are required for any online learning experience and teachers must choose among them for the best support of discussion and collaboration, but they are empty without the teacher and students developing actionable and interactive applications for them. Rheingold and his students connected through engagement tools like whiteboards, chat, and wikis. The students were able to communicate ideas and learn together at a distance, responding to one another as they saw their ideas take shape. The tool was secondary to the activities that had been established to encourage engagement. Rheingold described this achievement with an example of the students working together using a shared whiteboard, and noted that "words and phrases would appear on the screen and be shuffled around, and it was kind of magical. These are people all over the world who didn't know each other and had never met before, and it was instantaneously showing how to make a collective intelligence."

As Rheingold suggested, technology's capacity to make the learning experience visible is a powerful aspect of digital spaces. The engagement taking place in the classroom can be chronicled and returned to, providing students the opportunity to review and reflect on the work. Students can see how others are thinking and provide validation and encouragement. This experience can be opened to the class as a whole, or it can be used for small groups.

Margaret Terry Orr, professor at Fordham University's Graduate School of Education and chair of its Division of Educational Leadership, Administration and Policy, has her students work together on Google Slides, a web-based presentation application, and Jamboards, a web-based whiteboard application, to support collaboration and strengthen their understanding of the concepts being taught in the course. As she explained, "I establish several small breakouts and have each group go through different Google Slides featuring common questions, having them work through it together and reviewing each other's work, adding comments, suggestions, and changes. Other times, I'll create Jamboards and have each group go to a different board to work and again I encourage them to evaluate their work with each other, providing feedback, suggestions for improvement and so forth."

Orr uses these resources and spaces to activate meaningful student interaction and to produce a document of that engagement. This documentation provides an opportunity for teachers and students to review the learning that is occurring. Using technologies to collect snapshots of student efforts that are ephemeral in the traditional classroom, so that she and the students can (for example) return to questions asked during in-class discussions, has been powerful for Orr's teaching. She asked student groups to use Jamboards to work "on a single slide together so they can see the progression of what they're learning by the work being done on the Jamboards. So they can work and review together." Teachers and students engaging in online spaces can collaborate with one another through the display and recording of their thought processes, which provides the unique opportunity to reflect on their thinking as it is occurring and review what they are learning as it is taking place.

To spark engagement in the online classroom, and maybe any classroom for that matter, is to ensure that the students are not positioned to dutifully echo the answers that the teacher has given them. An engaged classroom online comes together as a community and everyone is encouraged to drive the learning forward through questioning and discovery. The seeds for engagement online are often sowed in discussion forums and video chats, systems intended for student communication and collaboration. In these spaces students are asked to engage with the class as a whole or in small breakout groups and have opportunities early on to adopt roles for engagement. These roles may be narrow, each student having a specific way to contribute to discussions and activities. Or their role may be more indistinct, where they are asked to collaborate as learners, sharing their thoughts and feedback as they watch how others learn from them and how they learn from others. They also document and record themselves engaged in these roles, so they can return to various moments in their learning experience and reflect on how they have grown.

TIPS

One thing that I did was I tried to balance the class time (so that students don't have so much Zoom fatigue) by creating these videos in Studio on Canvas, highlighting just some of the key points that I thought would be thought-provoking in some way. I would make a video and then have points throughout the video where they would pause and just comment on the prompt. So, I'd give some information, offer a prompt, and then they could comment on it. And what I've really loved about that is the asynchronous conversations that can happen. I think there's something powerful about students responding asynchronously, reading each other's responses and building on their own ideas. And for some students it's been easier for them to digest everyone else's ideas that way versus in person, when they're synchronously talking to each other. I've gotten a lot of positive feedback from students. Many of them are asking me how they can create something similar for their own students online because they felt it was very interactive. That's one thing that I really enjoyed. —Soyoung Park

ENCOURAGING AND SUPPORTING ENGAGEMENT

Sometimes even the best planning may not succeed in drawing engagement from every student. Students may do the bare minimum, completing only what is asked of them and doing very little else. This type of experience can be discouraging to new and experienced online faculty alike. The key to fostering meaningful engagement lies with the teacher. With the basics put into place, it is essential that the teacher be actively engaged in the learning that is occurring. The students must see the teacher as a member of the community who is present and available to them. It is equally important that the teacher is the force that drives the students to connect with each other and to the world in which they live. The teacher needs to be a model of engagement, providing constructs that bring students together. So what exactly can an online teacher do to encourage engagement?

For online engagement to be authentic, students need to see that the ideas they are sharing are being heard and that their peers understand what it is that they bring to the course. Teachers can start by helping students to get to know one another. Understanding who they are learning with is an important first step to creating a community that is truly engaged. A tried-and-true technique for helping students know who they are learning with is to ask them early on to share who they are. Many online instructors set up an introductory forum. In these forums, students are asked to share some details about who they are and why they are interested in the course. While you might think that this simple task would not do much for student engagement, Cali Morrison, "chief instigator and courageous coach" who runs an educational consultant practice called Creative Synapse, contends that even though "you may not get to see who the student is physically, you get to see who they are through their words and that helps to build relationships." In turn, she explained that these types of forums help to connect students. They may discover that "they're fans of the same team or that they have the same interest in disciplines." The small connections that happen in these moments generate authentic engagement online. As Morrison noted, "Finding those connections is important for building classroom community and it's fun to watch students find them in each other. They may have the same lived experiences, but didn't know they were crossing paths. It's neat to see those interactions happen."

Of course, online engagement is not just about the students getting to know one another. Online educators must also design classrooms that provoke and activate engagement. The engaged online classroom is more of a community space than a lecture hall. A community space depends on more of an organizational role, while the lecture hall depends on more of a performative role. The online teacher needs to be as committed as the students are to sharing thoughts and sparking collaboration. Langdon Graves, an artist who teaches at Parsons School of Design and Pratt Institute in New York, teaches a course in color theory online, and as she explained, she often shares current events that she personally finds interesting to inspire students to do the same. As she described, "Anytime there's some hot color news, I'll post it right away. For example, I don't know if you remember the huge debate about 'the dress' in 2015, whether the dress was white and gold or blue and black, but when it came up I thought, 'Ooh, I can turn this into a color theory lesson.' I would drop these tidbits of information and students would be curious and want to get involved." Graves's engagement helped to strengthen student learning and it also provided a model for how students could inspire one another online. Soon Graves discovered that the students were engaging in the same way, saying,

> "Oh, have you listened to this?" Or "Have you read this book?" They would drop their own suggestions for things to check out, which created conversations among them. It also was a way for them to look forward to learning about the class and applying concepts, like science, nature, and other things that are outside of a typical design class. It evolved into moving outside of the classroom and helping the students to reflect on something that's bigger than what we were learning at the moment.

The act of posting links to things of interest or making connections between class topics and complementary resources helped to inspire student engagement as the students were encouraged to seek out and share stories, ideas, and artifacts that were personally interesting to them and that helped to strengthen their understanding. They were encouraged to not just reflect on what the teacher was posting; they were also introduced to resources that influenced their thinking that others could also learn from, and that might in turn inspire others to share and reflect in a similar manner.

The orchestration that Graves conducts is no easy task as there is the potential for students to simplify the positive interaction she encourages, dumping resources and random thoughts into course discussions and activities to meet what they may perceive as a base requirement for assessment. In setting up online discussions that are open and flexible, Amy Lewis, faculty and program coordinator at the Graduate School of Education at Rutgers University, recommended that teachers do not overload the course with resources and materials; as she described, they

QUOTABLES

I never believed in "I'm just going to sit and talk to you for two hours and you're going to be grateful that you're in my class." I don't believe in transmission-based learning. I don't believe that my students are empty vessels that need to be filled. I have a different perspective, a different learning theory that guides me that is definitely more sociocultural and constructivist. Experiential learning that's rooted in the real world is important. And so I have students doing media making for three weeks about a topic that they're passionate about, but they've decided the topic, they've decided the genre, and they've decided the modality.
—Detra Price-Dennis

need to consider "narrowing the focus on what to talk about." By scaling back course readings and teacher prompts, Lewis encourages engagement through the opportunity for students to share their thoughts on the concepts being learned, ask questions of their peers, and learn from resources that help to strengthen understanding. She has found that leaving room for the students to add their voices to the lesson allows for a more spontaneous course experience, where the students are not just following the lesson but helping to develop it. Like Graves, she said,

> I read something new and I incorporate it into the course. This has been a big shift in my approach. I redesign my course over and over by adding something new to it on a regular basis. This has clearly been an opportunity for me to narrow my focus to what's really important. I've also gotten rid of some of the readings. I ask myself, Do I really talk about this in class? Is it really important? Or is it just that I like it and I've used it for a long time? If it's not worthwhile, then out it goes.

Lewis added that this approach, of discarding the old to make room for new, "forces me to learn new ways to present information and to provide greater access to the course and curriculum." By narrowing her content Lewis is making room for new and current ideas to unfold and manifest, opening more opportunities for the students to find ways to engage in class discussions and activities.

Modeling open and purposeful engagement as Graves and Lewis do is useful for understanding that engagement in an online course is not just the domain of the students, but of the teacher as well. As the course designer, the teacher must make room for new ideas and discoveries to be brought into the discussion and, as a member of the learning community, the teacher must be as excited as the students about what is being taught so that they too interject with new thinking and exciting developments. This may be more challenging than you might expect, as some teachers may have the mindset that online learning is a series of online modules consisting of text and videos that are developed one time and then imported over and over again and again, semester after semester. Caught in an endless cycle, the teacher may start to become uninspired by their engagement in the course, acting more like systems operators and less like encouraging and inquisitive learners. But as we have seen, the teacher's being appreciative of the students' curiosity and taking on the role of inquisitive learner helps to sustain student activity and engagement online.

Encouragement, which goes hand-in-hand with engagement, is the small nudges and kind offerings of recognition that helps students to see that their input has had an impact on the learning. What does encouragement look like? Cheri Gurse, former professor of undergraduate studies at Antioch University Santa Barbara, uses a post-class message to acknowledge the ways in which the students are engaging with one another and to say that their engagement is appreciated and valued. As she explained,

> In my message, I convey my enthusiasm for last night's class. "That was a great discussion!" Or "Here's what I got from yesterday," or "What you said reminded me of *this*." After these affirmations, I provide details or information such as "I left this out" or "Here's that link I promised." I repeat my invitation to be in touch with me. And I often include a cartoon or link to something fun—so there's warmth and there's information.

These small responses she described show the students how their engagement is positively impacting the class community and also model how to encourage others to engage in meaningful ways.

Finding ways to motivate students to interact with one another both inside and outside of the digital classroom is essential to engagement online. For example, group work is a useful tool for motivating student interaction. Group work and student engagement are inseparable, because the students have to communicate and collaborate with each other to complete the goals set for the group. Naturally, asking questions of your peers and listening to their feedback is an important aspect of any engaged classroom, but it brings added value to the online classroom because it makes student presence explicit and strengthens the idea that online learning is community learning. However, neither aspect is a given, as any teacher can tell you: Just because you get students into groups doesn't mean that the students will automatically engage in the work assigned, or become effective working groups. This is always a challenge, so it is useful to find ways for the students to empower one another to be more engaged.

One such approach is shared by Chris Friend, assistant professor of English in New Media at Kean University, who explained that the more empowered students are in all aspects of the group experience, including the assessment of the experience, the more opportunities there will be for engagement. As he explained,

> When students are working in groups, everyone in that group is aware of each other's contribution, and they understand how each student has contributed. And so I have the students evaluate each other in terms of how much the other students enhance their own learning experience and how others contributed to their ability to work through the material in this class. It is a big deal telling students that half of their grade comes from colleagues. It lets the students know that they are important and that they're not important for my benefit, but they're important for each other.

Empowering students in this fashion, helping them to understand how others may or may not be enhancing their learning experience, helps to make engagement tangible to the students and, following that, encourages the students to be more engaged themselves.

The approaches that we have shared demonstrate how teachers teaching online can motivate engagement by modelling it throughout the course, warmly acknowledging when the students are purposefully and actively engaged with the community, and excitedly displaying the kind of curious and enthusiastic interaction they would like to see occurring in their classrooms. While teachers can plan to incorporate these practices into their courses in various ways, such as announcements synthesizing mindful student responses and video blogs providing feedback on student efforts, this type of modeling is often intangible in the sense that it is more an extension of teaching practice than something built into the curriculum. However, we do not mean to imply that a more direct approach to engagement cannot be implemented online. In fact, clearly outlining for the students how they can be engaged learners online is a good tactic for encouraging purposeful engagement. In online courses it is often necessary to be clear in your expectations for how the students respond because they may be used to learning experiences where the act of being present is enough to be accepted as being engaged.

How can an online teacher be more direct in the solicitation of engagement? One approach is to ask the students to be as involved in the teaching as they are in the learning. This could be as straightforward as asking the students to take on the role of teacher and lead a class conversation in the forums or submit a reading for the students to discuss. Or it could be a presentation on the topics being taught or some other relevant knowledge that the students have acquired in their own right. As Lin Lipsmeyer, professor of teaching and learning at Southern Methodist University, suggested, "There are a lot of things the students learn and teach based on their own experiences that are amazing." To tap into this experience, Lin Lipsmeyer invited her students to teach a class on a subject

COUNTERPOINTS

I'm very interested in artificial intelligence. I feel like we need better systems to help students get more individually tailored feedback. It would be nice if there was a more AI-enhanced system faculty could use to give them feedback. Students make similar mistakes when they are writing papers and it would be nice if they could get feedback for those mistakes quickly. From the perspective of the faculty, it would be nice to have better data about the student. There's not a good system for faculty to know the patterns I'm describing. So I think using artificial intelligence in this way could help with engagement. It could help the teacher know more about their students, using artificial intelligence to recognize students' patterns, or some ideas that are recurrent in the students' work, and then provide immediate feedback. —Lin Lipsmeyer area that is known to them and relevant to the course concepts and content. Of course, it is not easy turning the teaching role over to the students. Lin Lipsmeyer pointed out, "There's always that resistance from students at the beginning and also doubt on my part. I would be worried if I was doing my job as the instructor; students would be worried if they were doing the right thing." And yet she has discovered that the students appreciate the experience, as it gives them the go-ahead to be more engaged in course topics, materials, and discussions. And her students agree: Lin Lipsmeyer noted that the week that the students teach is often the week they rate as their favorite. She added that the students comment that when they're invited to teach "they learn the most and they really understand the material much better." She explained further that when they're active in the learning and teaching "their voices are heard and this is when they are the most engaged."

Taking this approach a step further, Genevieve Lowry, who teaches in the Child Life Program at Bank Street Graduate School of Education, asked her students to be involved in the co-construction of the class curriculum. She explained that teaching online provides students with the tools to be active collaborators in the course content. "When the students share a resource to something they found online that means they did some research and that doesn't happen in an on-campus class quite as easily. It's not just finding it, it's also that the student thinks 'I'm going to share this with my fellow classmates because this is so easy to do.'" The opportunity for students in the online space to add content directly to the course supports the mindset that students are actively aiding in the construction of the course content and acting as partners in the learning and teaching.

ASSESSING ONLINE ENGAGEMENT

Even the most confident online teacher may still have some apprehension about whether these approaches will transform their online classrooms. While teachers may be eager to develop a more engaged classroom using the approaches we have shared, they may still be uncertain as to how to tell whether their students are truly engaged. Many educators still cling to assessing students' engagement by seeing them raising their hands, stroking their chins, scratching their heads, and nodding along attentively. In synchronous sessions, there is certainly some opportunity to keep that metric for assessment in play, but in a wholly asynchronous classroom, you are dependent on how active the students are with discussions, activities, assignments, and your feedback. Let us establish some understanding on how to think about assessing engagement in online spaces. What mindset should we have as online educators, and what signifiers could we use to measure the presence or absence of engagement in an online course? Identifying student engagement can be challenging, as Rodriguez Kerr explained:

> How do you know when engagement or inquiry is happening online? Well, how do you know it's happening in a face-to-face course? Is it the test score? I've certainly received high test scores on steps that I didn't learn very well when I was wearing my bad student hat. So it can't just be the test score. Is it showing up to a class? A lot of participation in face-to-face classes is just that you're there. Not that you've even said anything. It's just that you're sitting in the seat. It's a hard thing to measure face-to-face and it's an equally hard thing to measure online.

Learning online happens outside of a traditional classroom construct as some students engage in course discussions or activities while others are unaware that their peers are engaged at that moment. Teachers must look at student engagement as a collection of distinct actions that make up a whole. A lot of the assessment for an online course will be done using the same tools that one might use in an in-person course. Did the student respond to a post? Yes. Did they reply to someone else? Yes. However, using this approach to understanding engagement can go only so far. Student engagement is crucial to learning, and the need for students to understand when they are engaging deeply in the online space is important. Online teachers need to have clear language for when students are actively and meaningfully engaged in the learning experience. Sean Michael Morris, vice president of academics at online tutoring service Course Hero and founder of the online learning and teaching conference Digital Pedagogy Lab, provided a good analogy for this by comparing it to a student in an in-person course "who might jump into a seminar class, but has only been to lecture classes up to that point. They won't really understand how to participate in a seminar class because they think that they're just going to listen to the teacher." This is like the student who goes into an online course saying, "Okay, I'm going to post once, reply twice, like you asked me to, and that's all I'm going to do." If the act of engagement is nothing more than participation, then the danger is that online classes are seen as easy, meaning that the student engagement is perfunctory, and that rote actions and responses are enough. Morris goes on to state that "if we create a generation of learners who believe that teaching and learning online is something you don't really have to engage in or pay attention to, then we as teachers have really done something wrong." However, this is not a symptom of the technology, but of the teacher. It is up to the teacher to recognize and disrupt poor engagement. We need to change the things that students need to do to engage in the online classroom. Morris shared:

> They have to reconsider what kind of students they are. Because now they can't do what they normally do. That's a point of discomfort, but it also is a point where they can grow as learners. And they can recognize that something different can happen in an online space. The biggest barrier for me is the expectation

> that students come to online learning with a belief that teaching and learning online is the easy way, and it's just something that you don't really have to engage in or pay attention to.

If assessing student engagement is more than just checking boxes that students have posted and replied to forums and uploaded assignments, then an important step to assessing engagement is making sure that the students fully understand what purposeful engagement is. A teacher can do this by establishing norms for engagement around discussions, assignments, and activities. But it is not enough to simply establish these things, because students may not fully comprehend how to achieve the expectations for engagement. This is where the teacher can strengthen the student's understanding of what it means to be an engaged learner online, and in turn help the teacher assess whether the student is engaged in the course.

One way to help strengthen student understanding is to ask the student to speak about their engagement in the course. As Jesse Stommel, faculty in the writing program at the University of Denver, explained,

> The best way for me to know if my students are engaged is to ask them. So rather than saying, "Turn your camera on so I can see you," I can ask, "How did this work for everyone? Did everyone feel engaged today?" Or I can have students write about their own learning and their own learning process, talking to me and writing to me about how they're moving through the course. Ultimately, the way that I come to know if students are engaged online is just by asking them.

Asking your students to share how and what they are learning can deepen their recognition of their engagement and helps the teacher understand how engaged their students are in the learning process. A similar approach is the one Susie Rolander, faculty at Bank Street Graduate School of Education, took by asking students to record a short video response to demonstrate their engagement in the course discussions and content. The purpose of this is to help them reflect on how they've been engaged in the course activities and assignments. The questions she asked her students included, "What was the most powerful reading this week and why? What was your Aha! moment this week? What did you see on Twitter that was inspiring? Is there anything you want me to know that could help me help you as a student?" Rolander found that getting students to reflect on these big questions strengthened their understanding of engagement, which in turn helped her to understand how the students are responding to the ideas being taught.

In addition to providing students with a language to describe their own engagement and reflecting on whether it is meaningful, another way to assess student engagement is to look at how the students are engaging with the content developed for the course and also how students are working together as a community. While engagement in the online classroom tends to center on how the students are engaging with one another, there are other levels of engagement to consider, such as how students are engaging with the course content and materials. This is an important consideration online because the students are engaging with lectures, mini-lessons, prompts, and readings at their own pace, and the teacher has to make sure that this engagement is appropriate while not overshadowing the engagement between students, teachers, and other members of the learning community. This is why assessment of students' engagement with materials is important, as these materials help to strengthen the students' ability to reflect, respond, and reply to each other. The teacher must be aware of how the students are responding to these resources and refine them if the students are finding these materials to be overwhelming or obsolete. The more engaged the students are in the subjects being learned, the more engaged they will be with those around them. To assess this layer of engagement, Troy Pinkney, faculty and director of Programs in Child Life at Bank Street Graduate School of Education, explained how she uses the tools provided by the LMS to assess the extent to which students are reviewing the weekly wrap-up, a useful resource to synthesize student understanding and prepare them for the discussions and activities assigned for the next week.

> It's less important to know who is looking and more to know, is anybody looking? If I see one-quarter looking then I think, that's not working. I've got to do something differently. So, for example, I used to put the weekly wrap-up in the weekly module. But I think it was easier for people not to pay attention to that, so now I do it in two places: I put it in the announcement and in the weekly wrap-up. So there are multiple points for engagement. There's not one way to get this information—there are multiple points.

In her assessment, she discovered that the students were not as engaged with this resource as she had hoped, but instead of cutting it, she expanded the different points from which the students could access it. The flexibility of the online space allows faculty to test different approaches to engaging students in the activities and assignments of the online course. Pinkney uses the course technology to assess the engagement of students as a collective group. Less focus on singular student engagement and more on engagement overall helps to build opportunities for engagement at a greater scale.

Pinkney also makes clear that the data and documentation provided by the LMS add to the toolkit teachers can use to understand class temperature overall. Teachers can see across the students' work, which is documented and retained throughout the various communicative and collaborative spaces of the learning environment. This doesn't just include assignment submissions, but also conversations, validations, afterthoughts, links, and much more.

In an online course, engagement looks much different than it does in a traditional, in-person classroom. The way in which engagement is understood is changed when teaching moves online. The idea of looking out into a sea of faces to glean some sense as to whether the content is connecting with the students is gone. Even the immediate checkpoints of pausing to ask if anyone has any questions is gone. But we have also learned that this approach to engagement was never all that engaging in the first place, and moving online gives teachers the opportunity to better understand what engagement looks like.

In this chapter, we have presented a number of different practices and reflections from other online educators that can help us shift our perceptions of engagement for online teaching and learning. Along with providing some insights into the collaborative and communicative tools used to support student engagement, we have also looked at ideas that are transformative in how teachers perceive their own roles and the ways they develop curriculum for the online classroom. The most important of these ideas is the concept of the online classroom as a learning community. To inspire engagement, first and foremost, the teachers themselves must be as engaged as the students. This does not simply mean that the teacher is excited about the content they are teaching. It means that the teacher is an equal partner in the community as a learner. They use language that encourages further engagement and act as a model for what purposeful online engagement looks like. In the online classroom, the teacher is not the fountain from which all knowledge flows, but is instead one of many stakeholders working to inspire learning, albeit a stakeholder who is seen as being able to guide the class due to their experience with the content. The teacher also has to take on more of a role as a curriculum developer, someone who is able to organize different activities and actions and then manage those actions throughout the learning experience. The teacher is not just presenting content and ideas to the students and answering questions. In the online space a teacher has to be able to move through various points, responding to student needs and making sure to acknowledge when students are engaging and when that engagement is lacking. The teacher is no longer just developing a lecture, if they should ever have done that. Instead, they are developing points of action for the classroom community and they work within that community to ensure everyone is engaged and responsive. In this environment, where the care of the community takes precedence, the teacher also needs to have the capacity to assess whether students are engaged, and if not, then they have to look at the course as a whole and make adjustments to encourage engagement. While it may be enticing to think of the online experience as a digital book, printed and ready to be read and re-read over and over again, this is a false lens. Instead, the teacher must be able to review the assorted data points provided for the measurement of engagement, from pages read to posts submitted, and adjust the experience, constantly enhancing how students engage.

Ask Yourself

What is most engaging to you about your online course?

Who are your students and where would they take your online course if you let them?

CHAPTER 2

Inquiry

> Online, in order for real learning to happen, has to be people working together and sharing ideas.
>
> —Troy Pinkney

In this chapter we explore the online classroom as a space guided by inquiry where experiences are informed by student questions, interests, and wonderings. Teachers can adapt their lessons, activities, and assignments to respond to and expand the inquiry of the learning community.

INQUIRY TRANSCENDS ASKING QUESTIONS

In our experience, we have found that *inquiry* is an idea that educators feel great passion for, and that asking educators what inquiry means elicits many different perspectives. We define inquiry as the experience of seeking knowledge and understanding through authentic questions. Sometimes educators fall into the trap of thinking they are inquiring when what they are actually doing is confirming ideas or beliefs for which they already have their own answers or practices. Here, we assert that inquiry worthy of the name emerges from energetic engagement among learners supported by instructors, not from learned answers to prepared questions. Online classrooms guided by inquiry embrace the idea that while faculty bring expertise and content, student learning comes from the robust inquiry that occurs because of their inquisitive interactions with one another. Authentic inquiry promotes ownership

> **TIPS**
>
> If you have a sound pedagogical approach and an instructional set of practices, you can actually do a lot with basic tools. But if you have all the advanced tools and don't have pedagogy, it doesn't happen. It becomes easier when we frame it for faculty as, What is it you are trying to do? What is your goal? Then once you identify what the goal is, we think about what the strategy is to reach that goal. Then we will give you the tool. —Negar Farakish

of knowledge, champions myriad voices, and engages all learners (students and faculty alike) in seeing the work of the class as a mutual intellectual endeavor.

CENTERING THE ONLINE CLASSROOM IN INQUIRY

Dave Cormier said that the world "is almost entirely full of ill-structured problems, and training students for well-structured problems is the teacher-centered version of education, and training students for ill-structured problems is the student-centered version of education." Cormier added that we often think we are being student-centered teachers when we create choices, but these choices are still governed by our own perspectives. "What we're doing is creating a choose-your-own adventure, which is actually teacher-centered. There is a deep, underlying well-structured part of it, but we're trying to hide it under some ill-structured painting." Cormier does not teach that way anymore. He explained that he has a "much lighter touch now."

> This idea of an underlying structure that is about the preservation of my power is the hardest thing to deconstruct with students. And it's always the most important part of my practice. Once I can get that done, I can get the trust built up. They understand that there isn't a secret code that they're looking for, and that I actually want them to come up with ideas that aren't my ideas.

Cormier noted that this approach supports students in handling uncertainty and complexity since they will undoubtedly be confronted with it. We may experience frustration and pushback from students who simply want to be told what to do and how to think. A commitment to real inquiry asks us to trust that students can learn to embrace uncertainty and to understand that they will learn most deeply when there is not one right answer to a question. When students learn to pose questions for which there might not be definitive answers, and teachers learn to let go of the need to provide definitive answers and trust that the questions our students pose will deepen the learning of everyone, that is the foundation for an authentic inquiring environment.

> **FOR YOUR CONSIDERATION**
>
> I always get the question, "How do we show you we did the work? How do we prove to you we did this?" And I tell them, and I know this is strange, but I don't really care about you proving to me that you did this.
> —Jonathan Iris-Wilbanks

Successful online teaching and learning requires teachers to encourage and promote active engagement among their students, showing them that their input matters. A student-centered approach provides students with a gateway to enter the online classroom and to see themselves as contributing to the greater whole. Without the opportunity to make substantial contributions to the community, the students may begin to feel disconnected from their peers and to respond to discussions and assignments as though they are simply uploading information to a computer and not advancing the learning of the community through their own questions and understanding.

INQUIRY IN THE COURSE DESIGN

Genevieve Lowry explained that her program started out with too much structure because she was trying to take what she did on campus and transition it to online. Lowry acknowledged that this did not create the authentic inquiry experience she had envisioned. Assumptions that teachers make about on-ground teaching may not translate to online. For example, in Chapter 5, "Community," we will show that establishing a community of learners online requires an intentional action. In the on-ground classroom, the assumption (false or not) is that community development can be assumed to exist simply because the teacher and students share a physical space. Another example is how time is different online. In the classroom, questions about assignments can be asked and often answered at the moment work is assigned. That can happen online, too, if the experience is synchronous, but if the experience is asynchronous, precision and clarity in our assignments becomes essential. Lowry explained that teaching online expanded her pedagogy because in paying closer attention to how she brings her teaching practice online, she began to think about how students engage with one another and create authentic inquiry. Much of this change happened over time and required a willingness to look at her teaching "and let go of all of the expectations of on-campus teaching. There has to be a willingness to explore a learner's stance to developing our teaching practice online," said Lowry. Taking a learner's stance is fundamental for the encouragement of student inquiry online.

COUNTERPOINTS

Teaching online is more work than teaching in person, because in person I could wing a lot of things. I could say a lot of things that I wouldn't have to put into writing. I think there's more spontaneity in person that's like, "Let's just do this." Everything online has to be a bit more planned and everything has to be thought through, and everything has to be explained through audio or video or writing. It just takes a lot more time. But what I find the most valuable is that the graduate students that I've worked with said, "Working online has definitely improved my ability to provide effective feedback during class critiques." —Anna Divinsky

Authentic inquiry online requires us to consider more than teaching with prompts. Prompts are often a good starting point, but the inquiry is what happens after students reframe the prompts and pursue the questions they're interested in. We establish a culture of inquiry by having students pose questions that facilitate the learning of everyone in the class. As she adopted a learner's stance, Lowry engaged in inquiring about her online teaching using student feedback and her own observations of the interactions in the online environment.

Cheri Gurse considers inquiry an integral part of her online pedagogy. She explained, "It's important to me to convey knowledge in ways that enlarge students' perspectives, that affirm their entitlement to knowledge and their competence for exploration." She does this by creating "a mutual process for dialogue and inquiry so that students have multiple and diverse opportunities to experience and examine the world." For example, Gurse has integrated opportunities for students to respond to polls—often two or three times during a class period.

This was not a teaching strategy she thought to employ in the physical classroom, and she described her joy at discovering that creating these moments opened up opportunities for all voices—even the quiet ones—to be both seen (on the polling platform) and heard. Moreover, Gurse believes that these polls model a process of dialogue and inquiry because from the polls come additional questions or responses that go beyond the poll. In response to the inclusive invitation from Gurse—"What else do you want us to know?"—students often want to talk more about their own responses and others', and sometimes even point out the limitations of the choices offered in the poll. Polling is not only an opportunity to prompt student thinking; it is also useful for finding out what kinds of questions most interest the students. Teachers may ask students to identify whether they have alternative inquiries to the ideas being explored or they may ask students to comment on the questions being asked and whether they are useful to their understanding. Teachers may also encourage students to submit their own polls to better understand how the community is thinking about questions they may have. Polling should be one of the many tools that the community as a whole can use to collect information and stimulate inquiry.

Detra Price-Dennis, professor of teaching and learning and the director of Digital Education and Innovation in Teaching and Learning at Ohio State University's College of Education and Human Ecology, thinks about inquiry by asking what her goals are for learning. When she taught on-ground, the goals that mattered to her "would be around students bringing their own questions, having opportunities to talk about those questions and tensions around those questions."

Now Price-Dennis's classroom inquiry is not just concerned with the content and information of the course. It is also something students can bring to the online experience itself. Understanding how the online environment, or any learning environment, affects our experiences as learners is crucial. The better we are able to question the structures and spaces of the environment, the better we are able to question the learning that is occurring. In the online space, it benefits the instructors to become imaginative inquirers, which means students are able to consider What if? in their thinking and inquiry, and to see the space as what Price-Dennis described as "new worlds." She believes that this type of thinking and questioning can help the student and teacher to overcome any challenges that being online may generate. As she described,

> I do believe that the things I engage in, the media that I consume, whether it's entertainment or playing games, I feel like all of those things really do open up possibilities, like when you read books where you have to imagine worlds where people engage in world-building. So you have to imagine new terrains and new ecosystems and new topographies and new everything. And then you have to orient everything about this world to that world. And then you have to try to figure out how people make sense of that world and operate and function in that world.

She encourages teachers and students to be creative in how they prepare for the online space, helping them to better respond to distinctions between online teaching and learning from traditional learning. "Watch *Star Wars*. Watch *The Mandalorian*. Read science fiction, fantasy, or speculative fiction." Price-Dennis believes that this type of creative engagement inspires educators to rethink how they learn and provides them with the skills they need to question and reflect on the learning they're engaged in. As she explained,

> So this new world of Zoom and this new world of online to me is no different than going to the planet Hoth or thinking about the design of the Death Star. So I have to be able to think about what it is that I'm trying to accomplish and do under a particular set of circumstances and what the affordances are of the resources and tools that I have available. And that's what happens in world-building. So if you are immersed in those particular genres, I think they can't help but influence what you do in your pedagogy and what you do in instructional practices because you don't see limits, you see possibilities.

Price-Dennis clearly explained that this type of thinking can be useful for students and teachers who may be frustrated by their initial experience online, using this kind of creative reflection to solve basic issues that often come with, "Why doesn't the technology do what I want it to do?" She encourages teachers to ask, "How do we solve it? Not, Oh my gosh, I can't do this. This is horrible. My students won't turn on their cameras." Instead, she encourages a more generative approach. "Okay, let's all turn off our cameras. Let's all do this. And let's use the chat and let's use these different platforms where we don't have to necessarily look at each other, but we could still see how we're engaging." Price-Dennis offers the opportunity to turn an obstacle into a question and an opportunity for experimenting.

Counterpoints

When you're asking a question in the in-person classroom, you are limited to five minutes or so to pick a few students to respond, and that's assuming that you do it the right way, and everybody has a response. But online you have the perfect opportunity to hear everyone's thoughts. You can say "I want everybody to type their response in the chat." All 25 students within the same minute or two can contribute to the discussion, and you can look at it right then and there. You can identify a couple of those comments and call on those students to talk more about what they have posted. In my in-person class, we had a day of presentations and one of my challenges was how to engage the other students when one is presenting. I wondered what the other students were doing other than listening? How do I get them engaged? Throughout the years, I devised different strategies. I created a panel of judges, randomly chosen from among the students, and they would use the rubric that I would use for assessment without the grades. So they were not grading, but they were giving peer feedback. And sometimes I would have index cards. And I would ask the students to list a strength and an area needing improvement for each presenter, and then I would collect those cards and give them to the presenters. How am I going to replicate that in an online environment? Because if you have 20 people presenting, it can get boring after a while. I didn't know what the other students were going to do; they could just turn off their cameras.

I started thinking about that and I did two things. I said you're going to listen to the presentations and identify a strength and an area needing improvement to post to the chat for each presenter. Every person has to have a positive thing to say about this presentation and something that the presenter can do to make it better. Then I created a survey based on the rubric that I was using for grading and at the end of every presentation, I launched that, and the students started rating each other anonymously. These were opportunities for peer feedback. And then I graded the students' presentations. I put my feedback there and the grade that they received based on the rubric, then I included the survey results based on the peer feedback. And I copied and pasted everything from the chat for individual presenters. I then highlighted some of those comments the students had made that were in line with what I also had observed. And I emphasized that the highlighted sections were things that I thought they really needed to pay attention to because I observed the same things as their peers did. So the students had to think about all of these comments together. In-person, this would have been difficult, launching the survey, for example. Everybody would have to get on their devices. But online it's instant, and they're constantly engaged during a 5-minute presentation, they're jotting down the strengths and weaknesses. And then, at the end of the 4 or 5 minutes, they are done. And I show the results. Using the chat for class participation is less pressure on the students because you give everybody the same amount of time, and everybody has the same opportunity to say what they think. These are not quizzes or assessments. This is just to get the students to contribute their thoughts as they would in an in-person class. It's just that in an in-person class, you can't have all 25 students talking at the same time, but in the chat, they can.—Negar Farakish

Creating opportunities for inquiry requires all learners to step into a stance that embraces learning, to genuinely think and listen and sometimes leave behind what we already know in order to understand someone else's thinking. For this, teachers need to establish norms that let students see that their inquiries are as essential to the content as the instructor's. For example, in a math class, a subject that often elicits resistance to questioning in pursuit of one answer, one of the norms for collaboration is to listen with the intent to understand and speak with the intent to contribute. We believe that everyone wants to learn and if you tell them what you figured out before they figure it out, you stop their learning. It's not always easy. Learning is not a competitive sport and questioning what it means to question and probe someone else's ideas requires us to leave behind our own knowledge in order to make room to understand someone else's knowledge. This requires practice and patience.

Inquiry needs to be built into the design of the online class, inviting students in to question the direction of the work. Kristen Sosulski, clinical associate professor of Technology, Operations, and Statistics, and executive director of the Learning Science Lab at New York University Stern School of Business, feels strongly that a big component of course design is being explicit and clear about what you want students to do. "As educators, we're skilled at writing syllabi and providing directions and instructions." But she emphasized that in the online space, without practice, there may be many assumptions made that we are being explicit and clear. Simply providing direct links to information does not mean students clearly know what we want them to do with it. Sosulski thinks that instructors need to frame the work in explicit ways, which includes how the sequence of topics and activities are organized. But she adds that being explicit does not mean being directive. Her course evaluations were rated highly around organization and clarity and she attributes those ratings to how mindful she is about being explicit. "And when student feedback is telling me that it doesn't work, then I have an opportunity to grow and change that assignment or that project." She wants students to find their voice in the assignment and not approach the work as though it is a perfunctory checklist. "So that's a distinction that I'm making and sometimes I can go over to the other side by being too directive in the assignments, and sometimes I find myself having to pull back and acknowledge when I want them to struggle a bit." This struggle reflects good teaching.

For Your Consideration

I feel like the barriers for entering into a conversation are less online. My class was able to have 4-hour-long conversations where everyone was a cohost. Students could share something they wanted to bring into the conversation. So I might bring in a couple examples that I had, and we would talk about those in a theoretical and historical context and they would bring in relevant examples from their lives. They would bring in examples from TikTok and examples from other media that students might not traditionally bring into the classroom environment, but because we were in a digital space it was really easy to have that type of cross-disciplinary sharing in a non-hierarchical way.
—Amy Khoshbin

The online environment provides teachers with the opportunity to reconfigure the classroom. With the front of the classroom nonexistent, teachers are free to reconsider where their students focus their attention. Students can be guided to look inward at themselves and the community, taking the time to better understand themselves as learners and as members of a learning community. The ability to redesign and develop the online classroom into a more indeterminate space where students can move freely between their own interests in the course subject and the core concepts that the teacher is weaving throughout the space is at the core of online course design and development. However, even with the walls of the traditional classroom removed, students do need guidance, as their prior experience as learners may bring some trepidation to bringing their own questions into the space. So even in the weightlessness of the digital classroom, they need to be tethered to something. This is where the guide rails as described by Sosulski are relevant. Providing students with explicit pathways and gateposts, clearly outlining expectations for learning, and explicitly defining what learning looks like in the course and community can help students find the courage they need to be thoughtful in their inquiry in the online classroom.

STUDENTS AS INQUIRERS

A classroom where students' wonderings drive learning is key to supporting inquiry. And these wonderings support the teaching. Encouraging students to step out of the traditional role of just answering the questions teachers ask supports students in asking their own questions, thus deepening the learning for everyone. This is especially true in the online classroom, where students have more time to think about the knowledge shared and can deepen their own understanding and ask questions that can move the learning forward. Christina Katopodis, postdoctoral research associate in the Transformative Learning in the Humanities initiative at CUNY, prefers an online classroom where the students are the ones asking the questions. She does not think it is helpful for student learning for her to ask questions already having an idea of the answers she's seeking. "I much prefer students asking the questions. It's just a matter of structuring the discussion so that they feel they're in a good place to ask good questions." She also believes that this approach supports comprehension because sometimes students are confused by what they've read; through questioning, they support one another. "And that creates a sense of care in the learning community."

Amy Lewis believes that in order to create authentic inquiry, we need to think about who our students are. "Getting my students to think about who they are as learners through the lens of the content is embedded in an experiential learning environment." She believes that schooling often pushes unnecessary identities on students who think they're not science people, for example. Lewis believes that we need to ask ourselves why students have come to identify as not

Quotables

I have my students decide the medium and the audience. And the thing that I tell them every single semester, which is really hard for students who only see their professors [as their audience], is that I am not your audience. I get the privilege to give you feedback. And to evaluate you, that is a privilege, but I am not your audience. So, who is this for? Is this for your grandmother? Is this for the people on the corner? Is this for the kids in your community? Who is this for? It is not for me. So make something that matters to someone and then know that I will give you feedback and I will evaluate it based on the criteria, but it is not for me. I do not want to be your audience. So that takes the students a long time to understand, "Oh, she's serious." But it gets to this point that if it's experiential, it should be authentic. It shouldn't just be experiential. It should actually matter to someone for some reason, someone should benefit from this.

—Detra Price-Dennis

skilled or capable in certain subjects and she knows that starting from this experiential environment will support us in supporting our students to pursue inquiry. The most challenging course that Lewis has had to teach online was a science methods course. She explained, "It's such a hands-on subject by nature. I take pride in getting students to engage in science investigations and really do science collaboratively." She had to think deeply about how to create that inquiring learning environment without having all of the hands-on materials so that her students could still experience the course as a collaborative endeavor. The result? She developed investigation teams.

At the beginning of the semester, students were put on teams, and had to sign up

> for a week in which they were going to bring the materials to their team. Each week a different student conducted the investigation on screen at home so that their peers could be a part of the learning. One person has all of the materials and they're demonstrating in breakout rooms the actual experience for their small teams.

She goes on to explain that the work is approached as a collaboration because students make their own sense of the science and the experiment needed to prove the science. At the end of each lesson, she engages the whole class around a scientific phenomenon "and we explore it, develop questions related to it, and then they go into their investigation teams and conduct individual investigations. I try to create an experience where it's not only a demonstration but an opportunity for students to think about how they conduct the work as a collaboration."

In making student inquiry the focus of the online classroom, the teacher encourages students to observe and analyze themselves as learners while they engage in class discussion and activities. It helps the students see how they contribute to the learning experience in which they are taking part, and to see how each member contributes to the growing knowledge of the entire learning community. The collective understanding through inquiry weaves the students together, making the connection between them more meaningful, replacing the connections they make by sitting next to one another at a desk or in a class circle.

Online instructors may overload courses with too much content for fear of not teaching everything that needs to be taught, or that they may leave out an important reading and students will never know about it. However, this may hinder student inquiry as they end up seeing reading as a perfunctory task and not as an important activity for forming and strengthening their own knowledge and ability to ask questions about the course content. Teaching online, Troy Pinkney, faculty in the Child Life program at Bank Street Graduate School of Education, has learned that less is more. "In order to be scholarly, you don't have to read 20 articles a week." She finds that if there are too many readings, some students won't do any of them. This recognition impels "a kind of honing in on the readings, but also being very aware of what students bring to the learning, and for students to realize that it's not just my job to feed them content if the intention is to create a collaborative space." Pinkney explained further, "I could see the difference from when I assigned all these readings. Students weren't bringing them into the discussions, and now, offering more carefully selected readings, I'm seeing students include them in discussions, and not just throwing a quote in for show. There is evidence that students clearly read and thought about the reading. So I'd rather see students read less and actually refer to the reading and incorporate the learning into their assignments and reflections."

Providing students with structures that are more flexible offers more opportunities for them to reflect on the questions they have and the knowledge they are developing. This flexibility can include, as Pinkney suggests, fewer readings, which may encourage students to spend more time with the resources provided. Another approach to encouraging student reading is to create assignments where students are charged with finding, assessing, and presenting resources relevant to the class subject. Using the Internet as a resource to discover texts that offer answers to questions they may have helps to contribute to their own capacity as learners and also helps to engage them in the learning experience.

In the online environment, teachers may first think that their role is synthesis and feedback, which are essential elements of sound teaching. However, many first-time online educators may only offer feedback similar to grading a test or writing comments on an essay, rather than considering other approaches to encourage student engagement and inquiry, such as asking students to respond to feedback or having them offer feedback and synthesis. As an online educator, Kathleen O'Connell, professor emerita of nursing education at Teachers College, Columbia University, noted that she "spends a lot of time giving feedback to students online. I take a

Tips

One of the things that you have to do, from the very beginning, is to accept the fact that it's not going to feel the way it did before. It's not going to look the way it did before, and if something's not working it's not necessarily the students. It's how you are communicating with the students, and how you are asking them to communicate. You can't just do it the way it's been done before. You can still hold true to what you believe about teaching and learning but it's going to look and feel different, and I think as soon as I accepted that I was going to have to do things differently, I could still find ways to communicate to the students and stay true to the practices that I feel are beneficial to them. I don't feel like it's taken so much out of me to make this shift. —Amy Lewis lot of time to address things or say to them, Do you get that? Do you understand this?" She discovered over time that she is a better teacher when she's asking more probing questions that model for the students what questioning is, while taking a learner's stance herself. For example, explicitly asking students to reflect what they understand and what questions they continue to grapple with makes her feel better about her teaching. She acknowledged that getting students to ask questions can be challenging, sometimes like pulling teeth, and she also knows that engaging in inquiry is essential in online classrooms because it engages both the learner and teacher and helps to strengthen the teacher's ability to support inquiry.

Those of us who are immersed in studying, teaching, and learning online are developing a sense of what new questions we must ask ourselves in order to move this intellectual endeavor forward: How does learning online enhance the opportunities for authentic inquiry? How is inquiry taking shape now that the classroom doesn't have four walls? Appreciative Inquiry (AI) is helpful in embracing the challenge of listening deeply and in a way that nurtures deeper inquiry. Unlike a technical approach to teaching online or a list of things to master in order to teach online effectively, AI as a framework serves as a substantive thought process that focuses on identifying what works and analyzing how to do more of what works (Hammond, 2013). As we own and deepen our online teaching and learning, we learn to collaboratively inquire with an open heart and mind, and to be vulnerable and open to change.

The purpose of creating space for inquiry in the online classroom is to encourage students to take ownership of the learning. When students acknowledge themselves as learners and understand that their questions are essential to the knowledge of the community they are contributing to, they are ensuring that links are made between the teacher and student and that the learning taking place is not disconnected and singular. Adjusting the classroom away from teacher prompts toward student questions driving class discussions, teachers create the opportunity for a more flexible space, which can in turn make for authentic connections. Without this flexibility, we risk the danger of creating a confined experience, where the students may feel as though they are stepping through modules and submitting papers and questions to the teacher in an effort to demonstrate correct answers for garnering grades, not knowledge. Inquiry is the glue that connects learners and creates community, because a classroom steeped in inquiry means students are the center of the learning process and rely on each other to move the learning forward. While it may appear to teachers new to the online space that without the boundaries that usually come with traditional spaces things may quickly devolve, both Price-Dennis and Sosulski provide considerations for thinking about the digital space as a space that is conducive to change based on student inquiry and interest. The malleability of the online space gives teachers the opportunity to help students see their potential as learners as well as the potential of the online learning space.

Ask Yourself

As you design your online course, how are you making room for students' inquiry?
What aspects of your online course are guided by inquiry?
What questions do you have about your teaching practice?

CHAPTER 3

Equity

> And to those teachers who find online to be overwhelming sometimes, well, it is overwhelming, but if you believe in progressive education, there really isn't an alternative. If you don't somehow individualize, you're not going to be able to reach your students where they are.
>
> —Helen Freidus

In this chapter we explore how equity is essential to online learning and the importance of building an environment where all voices are heard, students have the opportunity to lead and guide discussions, and all learners support one another in ways that serve to strengthen learning and access to knowledge.

ELEMENTS OF THE EQUITABLE CLASSROOM

The discussion of equity around online teaching and learning is usually concerned with two areas: access to the classroom and all of its resources and the need for all voices to be heard. While in this chapter we will concentrate on the idea of all students being able to speak their minds and share their thoughts (and propose that the online environment provides a unique platform for the development of equitable space), ensuring students' access to online environments is also vital. As Clay Shirky explained,

> You could not get a conversation going about student access to technology before COVID. For years, I was banging my spoon on my high chair about the idea of digital natives being nonsense and people would humor me. And then COVID comes along and it's, What do you mean? You don't have Internet access at home? And the faculty were calling IT and asking, Can we get my student a hotspot?

The situation that Shirky describes is of the utmost importance. It is essential that everyone involved in the delivery of online education consider the inequity between those students who can and those who cannot access courses online. It is not enough to require students to have a computer and an Internet connection. Shirky observed that as more people experience teaching and learning online, the more they acknowledge that many factors can impact access to online spaces. He posited that it is critical to recognize, "What access does the student have to technology? What kinds of environments do they study in? What kinds of obstacles are they dealing with outside the classroom? Faculty can no longer wall themselves off from these issues." He argued that the faculty can't take the position, "I see the students 150 minutes a week. They owe me assignments. I'm sure they have lives outside of that, but I never give it a moment's thought." Shirky added,

> That's what I'm most excited about because this thinking is transformative. It's not enough to say that there are these well-worked-out digital practices, adopt them. Instead, it says to think about your students as whole people. And don't transfer these problems to student services because this stuff has a huge practical effect as to whether students will do well in their academic work.

Shawna Bu Shell, dean of educational services and distance learning for the Riverside Community College District in Riverside, CA, gave perspective to Shirky's appeal for developing a complete picture of the students when making considerations for learning online. In thinking about the challenges that students face regarding technology, connectivity, and space, she asked whether "onboarding for students into online classrooms may need to come with recommendations for how to put a backdrop on because your house is not in the right shape." For Bu Shell, to understand this access is to understand privilege because, as she noted, to be successful online you need a quiet place to work and it is "a privilege to have a space to work, a privilege to be able to shut the door from noise. All of that is privilege."

The challenge that this privilege creates for online learning is very much on display in synchronous classrooms, where students aren't just bringing their physical self into the learning environment, they are also bringing their homes and workplaces in. This is why when you are meeting students in these real-time spaces, you should offer a choice to the students, letting them decide when they want to be present by speaking and listening off-camera, and when they want to enter the online space as a whole person, bringing themselves and the world around them by being on camera. As Rena Palloff, longtime faculty at Capella University and Fielding Graduate University in California, consultant, and author of several books on online learning contended, students need the option to "select their level of inclusion in the online classroom." It is not, as she goes on to explain, that students are "disappearing" from their cameras; it is just that the students are selecting how and when they present themselves in the digital learning space. Of course, there's always concern that they are not mentally present, but then that is not something that can be gauged by physical or emotive presence alone. Jonathan Iris-Wilbanks, faculty and director of the Child Life program at Mills

College at Northeastern University in Oakland, CA, explained that the faculty must provide moments for the complete inclusion of students. He asks the students to

> think about the space they're in, in their homes, cars, or backyards. And I pair them up and, if they're comfortable, have them give a little tour of their space, or share some of the items that they keep around them in their home to keep them grounded or connected to their community and their family. The trinkets and the things that we keep around us. And I use that to build connections. So I ask the students to invite their partner into their space for a little bit, and say, "this is where I am right now," and the connections they've made with each other through this has been surprising.

For Your Consideration

Now the whole world has experience on how to work online. I think prior to this, you'd have some people that had facilities and other people who didn't. And so it would privilege those with more facilities. I think the pandemic leveled the playing field. We all have a basic sense of how to interact online and work collaboratively online.
—Margaret Terry Orr

The challenges that exist for students due to access should be an essential consideration for teachers as they embark on the development and design of equitable classrooms; however, our goal is to provide insight into practices for online classrooms. What follows will be a look into some different approaches that teachers might consider when seeking how to create equitable classrooms, where the students are able to see that their questions are being answered, their ideas are being heard, and that they are having a real impact on the learning they are engaged in.

DESCRIBING THE EQUITABLE CLASSROOM

Understanding how to design equitable online spaces means understanding the inherent power structure of any classroom. Amy Khoshbin, an artist who has taught at the University of Nevada–Reno and at Pratt Institute in New York, pointed out that the traditional hierarchical classroom structure of teacher and students doesn't easily lend itself to the fostering of equity. She calls attention to the existing challenges of the real-world classroom, in that "there's a power hierarchy in the way the teachers will stand and the students will sit. Even having everyone sitting in a circle doesn't change this dynamic because the teacher may be projecting something on the wall and everyone's looking at it and engaging with it." The impact of online learning, especially synchronous teaching and learning, is that there is a leveling of the teacher and the student. As Khoshbin shared, "What I find amazing about Zoom is the non-hierarchical space it provides, where everyone is an equal talking head." While this disruption of traditional structures is inherent to online classrooms, she admits that this is not enough for the establishment of an equitable online learning space. She added, "For learning that truly feels equitable and that truly feels inclusive, it needs to be a space where the students can be vulnerable, can be themselves, and can bring whatever from their lives into that environment and have that be part of the learning experience." While establishing this type of classroom takes effort, being online can offer varied pathways for being heard, providing students with multiple tools for adding their voice to the class discussion and projecting that voice from the space they exist in and learn from.

Because the digital space is a non-space, understanding the whole student means understanding the tangible spaces from which the students engage. It is essential that instructors work to understand these spaces, because as Shirky noted earlier, the idea of the digital native has permitted instructors to assume that learners from younger generations simply know how to exist in the online space. However, while many students may step in and out of different digital spaces daily, they may not have a grasp of what it means to learn in an online space. *Learning* online is a different experience from *being* online. Students may be using various devices to consume, create, and curate content on different social media sites and apps, but that experience is wholly distinct from being an online learner. Teachers teaching online should not assume that they are less savvy with technology just because the students entering their classrooms use technology more frequently.

In the same line of thought, teachers should also not assume that just because students have had online learning experiences they are strong online students, because their previous classes might not have left them with a deep understanding of what a robust online learning experience requires. As an online teacher you should not discount your role as helping your students understand what it means to learn online. Not only does online learning provide an opportunity for teachers to reflect on their own practices—it also helps students reflect on what it means to learn and to better process the educational experiences they have in the online classroom. An example of this is the "life stream" project that Jeremy Knox, faculty in digital education at the University of Edinburgh, has developed for his online course. A life stream is similar to a blog, or an online notebook, as Knox described it, where students "set up little bits of code like an API, which allows the blog to automatically record what they do on the web. So if they like a YouTube video or if they favorite a web page, then that automatically gets attached to their blog." Knox explained that the purpose of this assignment was to demonstrate to the students that

> When we engage with digital technologies, we're spreading ourselves across these different technological agencies, and in doing so they lose a bit of

> themselves. That's the important thing I try to teach my students because I find that so much of the discourse around education, particularly educational technology, is that we're always trying to put students in the driving position, to take technology and use it to enhance their learning. So that agency is all on the part of the students. And one of the things I try to convey is that when you start to engage with these very powerful technologies, particularly the kind of data-driven software that underpins the web, these systems have agency over what we do. The life stream embodies that because it's automatically adding things and it feels out of control. And for me, that reflects the experience of trying to learn on the web, where you're not always in control of what's happening.

The system Knox has designed helps students to better understand how they present themselves online and how that presentation of self is dictated by the systems they use. Drawing the students' attention to the impact technology has in their daily lives helps students to appreciate the online learning experience and how systems influence their comprehension.

For teachers, finding opportunities for students to understand themselves as members of and learners in online spaces, whether those experiences are positive or negative, is crucial to the design of equitable classrooms. Teachers need to make clear that the digital spaces students will use and visit throughout the course may not be equitable. So it is important that in the design of classroom spaces students are aware of the mediation that may be taking place and know they can comment on the challenges it is causing and suggest ideas for adjusting the borders to be more inclusive, if they are constrained. For classrooms to be equitable, teachers must provide opportunities for students to understand equity and what makes an equitable online space.

DESIGNING AN EQUITABLE CLASSROOM

It is important that, as teachers, we are consistent in our commitment to equitable classrooms. In designing these spaces, teachers should look to understand how the students are communicating with one another throughout the experience and use what they find to build practices that support equity. When we make equity a central aspect of how we develop and assess class activities, we strengthen our own grasp of what equity looks like in the online classroom. Jessica Blum-DeStefano, faculty in the leadership programs at Bank Street Graduate School of Education in New York, asks herself throughout her teaching how she ensures that she is serving all of her students. She found that frequently asking this question keeps her focused on designing an equitable classroom. As she explained, "That's something I work on a lot, just my own development, my own consciousness, my own racial literacy, my own ways of facilitating those kinds of things in mixed groups. It is important to invest in the development of myself and my class development—that's neverending." Classroom equity depends on teachers striving to better understand how students are included, especially with online classrooms, where those spaces provide multiple ways to post and reply, to gather and break out.

> **Tips**
>
> I gave my students an assignment to build a ramp and present the ramp to the class synchronously. They found a variety of materials: some books, something that rolls, and a timer. It was actually funny to see all the different things that they brought and what they used as ramps: some of them had wooden ramps, some used binders. So they could use everyday materials that they would find around their home, which to me is a connection to how you bring science home to your students, leverage the materials that they actually have at home, and do that intentionally so that everybody has access to science and these investigations.
> —Amy Lewis

By establishing online classrooms where students are able to appreciate the opportunities for equity and accept that traditional structures may be discarded in an effort to create more communal and shared learning spaces, teachers can start to introduce circumstances where the students may be involved in the development of the course itself. Learning online offers the class community a chance to survey and gather input on the structures and expectations of the course and then respond accordingly to what they have discovered. When encouraging this type of action from students, Christina Katopodis recommended adopting a "no such thing as a universal syllabus" approach, adding that we "give choices to the students and ask them to engage in making those choices with you." She shared that because of this approach she provides the student more "ors."

> You can do a midterm paper *or* you could write bi-weekly reading reflections that are lower stakes and not graded. Giving students these options has really helped. I had a student whose father got extremely ill and it was really hard for her to manage the reading reflections. So she chose the midterm option and was able to stay in the class. She did well in the class and succeeded in the end even though she missed a couple weeks because she needed to be close to her family. So ors add a degree of flexibility to your syllabus. They also account for neurodiverse learners.

Establishing a variety of opportunities for equity and fairness throughout the learning experience in the online classroom aids in the inclusion of all students. The more opportunities there are for students to introduce their voices and ideas into the design of the course materials, the more equitable the experience can be overall. As Katopodis noted,

> Embracing choice and inviting students into making choices as cocreators is incredibly important. It takes trust and it takes listening and it's absolutely worth it. And I think it makes the syllabus more equitable. I think there are just some things we can do as the authority figures in the classroom to share some of that authority with our students and to help students reach the level of autonomy and independence that they're going to need for the rest of their lives.

In the online space, it is good that the students understand what it means to be part of a learning community, especially a community that is digital. This will only strengthen their own confidence to be involved in the classroom beyond the role of student and undertake the various actions needed to inspire community engagement and to take ownership of their learning. Using the online space to help dismantle the hierarchy of the classroom offers students a chance to see themselves outside of the teacher–student dynamic, giving them more opportunity to see themselves as community members, individual students, and classroom leaders. Being able to take on more of a role in how the class is formed and delivered may bring with it some questions as to what the role of the teacher looks like in an equitable space and how that role is connected to the role of the learner. One place a teacher could begin to explore this in their practice is by ensuring that the community members have equal access to the teacher as a community resource.

While it is often argued that the mediation of the learning experience online makes the teacher appear more distant, there are ways that online augments and enhances the teacher as a resource for feedback, discussion, reflection, and synthesis, and that is the teacher's ability to be available to students, whether one-on-one, in small groups, or as a whole classroom. Margaret Terry Orr provided a great example of this in describing how she supports doctoral candidates online. She starts her class by discussing logistical issues with her students and then she puts them into individual breakout rooms so they can write. She explained,

> I'll go door-to-door and check in on them. And sometimes they'll meet with each other or we can do just-in-time mentoring on where they are. We can handle things in 10 or 15 minutes and they keep going, but I may go back to them two or three times during a 4-hour period, but they have a 4-hour writing block. And we do this week after week.

Orr ensures that the students are getting access to her; she also identifies issues that are affecting everyone, and, as she noted, "if there's a question or problem that involves the whole group, I can bring them back from their groups and talk about something." This availability and immediacy is valuable for doctoral candidates, who may not always have the time and access necessary to complete their writing. This type of support would be valued by most students in any learning situation and Orr argued that this constant, direct contact would be "impossible to do face-to-face, just impossible."

It is also the teacher's role to help the community understand that the learning environment is a safe space where voices can be heard openly and ideas can be shared freely. Michelle Pacansky-Brock (https://brocansky.com/), faculty mentor for online teaching and learning through the California Community Colleges' California Virtual Campus, explained that it can be challenging to help students feel they can be open and share their voices freely within learning management systems because "there are no cues of safety. If anything, it's what scholars would call an ambiguous space because it could say welcome but then there could be other cues that signal threat." In developing her online space, Pacansky-Brock works to "reduce equity gaps and create an environment that is welcoming and supportive of all students." She thinks about "cues of social inclusion," or as she explained, "trying to be intentional about bringing in kindness and using supportive cues to demystify what success looks like." Something that Pacansky-Brock does to set this tone early on is send a video of herself to signify that the learning space is safe for learners. She described the video as "me in my backyard that I recorded on my phone. It's not perfect. I want them to know I'm not perfect and I'm not going to expect them to be perfect. It's less than a 2-minute video and I just want them to know that I love teaching. I want them to know that I'm here for them, that I'm in this with them. And that I'm flexible." Teachers can signal that the online space is welcoming and inclusive, helping to acclimate students to the environment and giving them a sense of ease and confidence.

In spaces for online learning, developing norms for equitable voices and engagement strengthens students' understanding of what it means to be engaged in a community for learning. Online teachers and students need to be explicit in establishing the online learning space as a communal space, because they will not have the advantage of physical proximity to bond the class together quickly. With the online classroom, the concept of an open community may be the best approach to creating an equitable learning space, where the members of the community have a say in determining the goals and outcomes of the community. However, it is not enough to simply state that all voices

> **QUOTABLES**
>
> I don't know what it's like to teach online in a world not in crisis. But for me, I think that the world being in crisis and teaching online forced educators in the Academy to reckon with the lived experiences of students in a way that they had not had to face before.
> —Christina Katopodis

must be heard to create an equitable space. Community online is more apt to take root if the students understand that there are multiple ways for them to enter into the learning experience, beyond teacher prompts and forum posts. They also need to understand that it is appropriate to be a leading voice for learning and that in the online environment you do not need to wait for a teacher to prompt you to speak. Students need to know that they have access to the faculty teaching the course when they need them, using asynchronous modalities to share thoughts and to connect with voices both inside and outside of the classroom. This type of access provides students with the opportunity to confirm thinking outside of the group and emboldens their voices, giving them the confidence they may need to be active class leaders. This type of equity can be challenging for teachers who are used to being at the center of the classroom. Online courses that emulate the model in which the teacher is the central voice and can only be accessed at select times of day may keep students from getting involved in the course beyond basic responses to prompts and uploading assignments. But the idea of students helping to lead the class, and even adjusting the flow of the course, is disruptive even for seasoned educators. Students may not be used to seeing learning as communal, only having experienced a model where the teacher is presenting knowledge to the students and the students are responding back to the teacher with the right answers. Online teachers need to make their intentions explicit to encourage learning that comes from the entire community of learners.

The equity that comes from inviting each student to speak up and interject is essential to online teaching and learning. In the online space you can understand each learner distinctly, and not fall into the trap of the classroom as a homogenous group of thirty heads providing single answers to questions posed. Instead, online courses can provide opportunities for teachers to "honor the reality of individual people's lives," as Helen Freidus, former faculty in the Bank Street College Reading and Literacy Program, put it. For example, she noted that in the asynchronous online space, "Students don't have to be available at 10 o'clock on Tuesdays and Thursdays. The teacher can work to find a time that's mutually workable for the student, and that makes a big difference." But the realities of people's lives aren't just based in time, as Freidus noted. "Online teaching and learning provides opportunities for individuals to enter into learning where they are developmentally, culturally, psychologically, economically, and to grow from there."

Finding ways to open access for each individual student in the online classroom does not need to be complex, just considerate. B. Stephen Carpenter II, dean of the College of Arts and Architecture at Penn State University and a professor of art education and African American studies, provided some easy-to-achieve ideas for ensuring how online teachers can provide ways to reach all learners because, as he noted, "online can provide equitable modes of access and communication for all students." For example, he recommended that for "the shy student, who doesn't necessarily have the confidence to speak up, give them access to the chat." Susie Rolander echoed Carpenter's assessment, as she has worked with students "who wish they could talk to me, but they don't have that kind of personality." To make sure these students have an impact in the course, she uses video check-ins, providing each learner "their own time to share what they are thinking about, because they know what the questions are and they can make some connections and then I can say, 'I understand why you thought about this and I'm wondering what you think about this.'" Also, like Carpenter, she uses chat to make the classroom discussion more accessible. If she finds a student is "worried to ask a question because they feel like they should know the answer and other people have more understanding," she responds by inviting the student to send her a direct message in the chat and then she asks their question of the class. For Rolander, access to these communication tools creates an opportunity where "people have equity in terms of having their voices heard," and for her that "feels really powerful." The pathways that the tools provide allow for various learners to find new and meaningful ways to share what they know with the teacher. Negar Farakish, assistant dean and clinical associate professor in the Division of Programs in Business at the NYU School of Professional Studies, provided additional insight into this experience:

> An issue for an in-person class, or even a synchronous class, is that if somebody has a question, then they must raise their hand or vocalize it. And some students feel a great deal of peer pressure. They want to look smart in front of their peers. And I hear this all the time from students, that they're afraid that what they may say is not smart enough. They think to themselves, "What are my classmates going to think about me?" But I use that as a strategy and tell them that I am monitoring the private chat and if you are not understanding, if you want to give me another example, or if you want me to clarify something, send me a direct message. They don't want to raise their hand? They don't want to put it in the public chat? Use private messaging to ask me without saying anything publicly. And I share this with the class by responding. Let me give you another example. I don't add "because Sarah didn't understand this." I just give another example to make sure everybody understands what's being talked about.

With this approach, all students are able to share their thoughts and understanding. In an equitable classroom it is not just about sharing correct answers, it is also about sharing questions, concerns, confusion, and even wrong answers. Farakish succinctly explained, "The expectation is simply that they contribute."

The online environment provides pipelines for students to connect to various community peers and leaders, as well as experts and other institutional thought partners in real time. An example of this is the student emailing the teacher with an idea or question in the evening or while they are in the field experiencing something that connects to the course content. In return, the teacher provides feedback and resources to the student directly, and also to the community as a whole, through an announcement or forum post. Giving students the freedom to speak without apprehension and when inspiration strikes is a very powerful tool for teachers, who can guide the students at various levels of understanding in the moment learning takes place.

Freidus acknowledged that the capacity to increase one-on-one engagement can allow for more opportunities to provide direct access not only to students and teachers, but to crucial resources outside of the classroom. This may be someone seen as an expert in some area, or else just someone with similar experiences or backgrounds. Freidus provided an example of this type of access, sharing the story of an international student who had a lot of trouble finding work in the United States, but managed to get a job as a security guard. However, in his home country he was a florist. The teacher who was working with him on reading, writing, grammar, and language managed to find somebody who was a florist in the States to help him learn the language of the profession in English, to prepare for interviews, to think about the links between his culture and American culture, to convey his knowledge of plants and to build on that.

With this example, Freidus shared two layers of equity. This student was given access to a crucial resource to help him find the work he wanted, and the teacher was able to "take the curriculum components and recast them in an individual way so that he could still earn a living and see other opportunities for himself." So, in this sense, the teacher not only provided direct support to the individual student in the online space, but she also did so while respecting the real-world time and responsibilities of the student.

For Your Consideration

I think that for me understanding different ways of creating intersectional dialogue is much harder to achieve in a place-based learning environment, because I was doing these Zoom events, or performances, or gatherings, or maybe dialogue conversations. It's funny, there's not a language for it yet. "Zoom event" is really terrible because it's just like a branded experience, which is horrible, but I was doing these, you could say performances, but they're almost more like town halls. That's also not quite right. But this experience made intersectionality possible. I would bring in city council candidates and folks from the electoral realm. I would bring in people who were organizers working in the spaces of mutual aid, abolition, et cetera. I'd bring in artists, creative practitioners, and educators from across the U.S. to be in dialogue with one another and with the participants online. We did these events in different formats—dating shows, participatory healing actions, creative digital collage-making sessions. We could do this in an in-person lecture series, but the expediency of online gatherings—which is actually an unhealthy problem where you have a million meetings back-to-back—can also allow someone who may have a very busy schedule or different life circumstance to tune in and participate for an hour, if you're looking on the positive side of things. Someone could easily share their knowledge, and get back to their lives. And we can all have an ongoing conversation before, during, and after the event no matter where we're located. It was so powerful to have entities from all these realms in dialogue with one another. For example, it really brought the conversation around abolition home to the younger generation, who may hear those words, but not understand what they mean until they're directly speaking to someone who's organizing in that space and/or living that horrible experience of the prison industrial complex. It's easy to tune out another social justice buzzword. But if you make the experience of learning about a topic fun, engaging, absurd (in the context of a dating show, for example), it's a different story. If we meet people where they are, it can activate and inspire folks to create change. We were able to do that because of the flexibility of the online platform. The ongoing online dialogue is one way to create coalitions and move towards diversity and social change. We can converse and work with people who might not be able to show up in person for a variety of reasons, but they can tune in on their phone for an hour, learn, have fun, and make connections. And so these online platforms can be a powerful tool to unpack. What I just described also sets the stage for those conversations to potentially be deeper because as we transition to in-person spaces, because the dialogue has already started, they can be sustained in person and continued from wherever we're located in the world.—Amy Khoshbin

From these examples, you can see that teachers are constantly seeking ways to engage students who are concerned about not being appropriately informed, not having the same access to resources or knowledge as their peers, or saying something that may not be received as intended. The inequity that these feelings can create means that there are types of students who will dominate in settings that mirror the practices of an on-ground lecture. These spaces are narrow and allow for only a certain type of learner to fully engage. However, the amplification of pathways to communicate and share that the online classroom offers increases the opportunities for all types of learners to respond and be heard.

For an online classroom to be equitable, as Kristine Rodriguez Kerr argued, faculty must adopt a multimodal approach, which she described as "trying to see which students are responding to what type of modality and getting them to produce assignments in multiple modes so that you can celebrate their strengths." She explained that in her practice, she tried to avoid creating "barriers to participation or . . . valu[ing] one type of participation." Instead, she tries to "think about multiple layers of acceptable participation." Rodriguez Kerr added,

> I try to find some type of communication that the student feels comfortable with and that's hard. It's hard to do well in any course, face-to-face or not, but in an online course where it's easy to reduce everything to reading and posting, you have to actively think about how I am inviting the student in. And if they underperform, then where's the place where I can create a balance so that they feel like they're welcome in the space, even if they're not great at this one type of activity?

By finding and understanding the different ways that students can enter into the course, Rodriguez Kerr has provided a level of fairness that allows for all students to find success in the course assignments and activities. She provides an example of how one student, who had difficulty engaging with the class readings online, had to find an alternate way to be successful in her course. As Rodriguez Kerr shared,

> I had a student who had a really hard time processing written texts and so they used software that would read PDFs and forums. They had some screen reading software and they found the audiobooks of course textbooks online. And they needed the encouragement to know that it was okay to do it this way, to find a way in. I think this student would have struggled in a face-to-face program, trying to figure out that this was the way they needed to learn. But I'm always thinking of the students who would be excluded, and how I make them feel welcome in any space, but particularly an online space.

Encouraging the students to better understand how they learn in the online environment (or any environment, for that matter) can help to create a more equitable space. With the online classroom it is useful to adopt a multimodal approach to teaching and learning, as it helps

> **TIPS**
>
> So here I am trying to do an AnswerGarden [a free feedback tool] and it doesn't work, but I had post-its, I had a back-up. I can still build consensus and show where we all are with post-its. It doesn't have to be a tech tool because the goal was to show what everybody was thinking in a way that allowed anonymity, allowed people to interact with the content and allowed for us to have a visual. What are the objectives? What would it look like face-to-face? What would it look like with the tools synchronously and asynchronously?
> —Detra Price-Dennis

learners take into account how they like learning and to strengthen their own understanding of themselves as a learner, both online and in general. By helping students understand themselves as learners, teachers help to inspire student voices in class discussions.

What is the goal of the student seeking to learn online and how can online learning provide access? Understanding why a student may not see the need to travel to a building for their education provides an opportunity for teachers to see the student as a whole person. Jesse Stommel noted that he came to online learning reluctantly at first, but his hesitation changed to enthusiasm as he started to see how access to his online class opened up new learning possibilities for his students. He explained, "I was working with students that I would never have been able to work with in any of my face-to-face courses. I had soldiers stationed in Iraq. I had a mother who lived in a rural area over 80 minutes from the nearest college or university. I had a student who was chronically ill and couldn't go to class in person." The barriers created by physical space and distance can be reconsidered in the development of an online classroom. Learning online opens opportunities for increasing who can contribute their voice to the learning experience, and the design of the course should provide opportunities for the students to share not just who they are, but also how they are coming to the space. In doing this, students may become more comfortable in presenting themselves, inspiring each other to find connections. This openness and accessibility is also inspirational to the teaching of the course; as Stommel explained, understanding where his students were coming from encouraged him to figure out how his students "persist and exist" in online classrooms.

Understanding that the strength of an online space is in the potential to hear all student voices and to more clearly engage each individual student brings with it the need to understand the diversity of the class and how the teacher can respect and acknowledge that diversity. Iris-Wilbanks does what he described as "monitoring the intention in the conversation." He explained,

When everyone is together in the online space and someone asks a question that is very

> personal about what somebody shared, I step in and point out how that question was intensely personal and then give the person who was asked to reply the chance to not feel like they have to be on the spot to answer. So I am monitoring those instances where there might be microaggressions or someone might be overstepping a boundary of what another student wants to share. And I've really noticed that these are moments where students turn on their cameras and lean in to really listen to what somebody is sharing about how they're processing the information or the content of the class. And sometimes there are

> long silences, and I try not to break the silence for them, but to let them sit there on Zoom together until somebody shares.

The ability for the teacher to acknowledge the diversity of the students in the classroom and to ensure the comfort that all students need to share is important to the development of a respectful and equitable online space.

DEFINING AND CREATING EQUITY ONLINE: IDEAS TO CONSIDER

Recognizing the diversity of the students in the classroom and providing opportunities for them to recognize and learn from that diversity is crucial for encouraging students to bring their whole self into the online learning space. We should create spaces that give students the ability to bring not just their academic selves, but also those intimate aspects that may hinder (or impel) them to be authentic in the learning space, such as emotional traits, socioeconomic status, ethnicity and race, and personal beliefs. This is what it means to accept the learner as a whole person. Establishing different ways for students to interact with the learning community so that their distinct voices can be heard is essential to an effective online classroom, where the student does not feel disconnected or ignored. Building such a space online may sound daunting, and yet the practices shared by the educators we have spoken with provide a good foundation for adopting practices that take advantage of the digital space as an equitable space.

The approaches that online teachers can embrace to inspire student equity in online classrooms depend on their recognition of those spaces as being more effective when they are communal. They are spaces where the teacher's voice is not dominant, but guiding, supportive, and affirming. With the online learning space, there is an opportunity to level the traditional hierarchy of teacher and student, setting up spaces where students may lead the discussion, offer course resources, and speak to their own experiences. The dominant voice is a community voice in the online space.

It is also important that students understand what it means to be one's self in the digital environment. Too often students may see online learning as a transaction, where they complete activities and submit assignments without any need to engage with their peers, similar to experiences they may have on social media, where they are blasting out content to a faceless mass for likes and retweets. It is important that throughout their online learning experience they are provided with opportunities to explore and question what it means to learn online and what online learning means for them. They need this so that they can better understand how to bring their voices into the online community and to better understand who they are as learners.

To develop that sense of online voice, teachers need to adopt a language that supports inclusivity and honors individuality. The stories shared provide a variety of different approaches to consider for online learning, such as providing opportunities for learners to select their level of inclusion and understand what an equitable online space looks like; synthesizing learner responses collectively, so they can see the impact their voice has on the whole class; encouraging learners to bring their whole selves into the learning experience; opening multiple pathways for learners to add their voice, such as forums, blogs, breakout rooms, and chat; creating flexible course materials, such as syllabi and models, that allow for student input; and, as a teacher, making one's self accessible to the students at different times using the different tools available. Using these various pipelines for communication lends itself to the service of the diverse engagement needs that all learners have.

> **Quotables**
>
> For me personally, I do feel in some ways that I can make this more of a curated production and that's kind of how my mind goes. When I'm thinking about a Zoom class, it's not, "Well, let's log on and see where it's going." I have my plan on cards and I can move them around depending on where students are with content. And I do think that it's been enjoyable to curate the class in that way and to bring them along and create connections and then go into content and then process and use the breakout rooms. —Jonathan Iris-Wilbanks

These same tools also expand the pathways on which students are able to access peers, groups of learners, and teachers. While opening these pipelines may seem intimidating for teachers, who may be more used to the classroom existing as a limited amount of time with one or two pathways for communication, the ability for students to reach out to internal and external resources is a real opportunity, making sure students have the access to the things they need when they need them. It also makes it possible for students to bring resources and voices that are representative of their own thinking into the classroom, strengthening who they are as members of the learning community.

The design of the equitable online classroom enables the community to adjust the flow of the course structure as new and inspiring ideas are formed. If the students find something that enlightens the class as a whole and strengthens understanding overall, then that knowledge should be able to find its way into the class. For this to happen, the teacher must be willing to be a part of the community as a learner, helping to guide and encourage ideas. The students must feel supported in these efforts and be able to share with the teacher what they have found and to get feedback on how to bring that thinking back into the classroom. In learning online, providing students with the tools to add and dissect ideas is essential. These tools help to amplify personal vision and voice, and because the online classroom is often a document of the student's experience, this means that the students not only feel a sense of having learned, but a sense of having created learning for the community they helped to shape.

Ask Yourself

As you design your online course, how do you account for all voices, including your own?

What aspects of your online course welcome different ways of engaging and celebrating different strengths?

What do you do to support students in bringing their authentic selves into the classroom?

CHAPTER 4

Presence

> My experience online, which I often complain about to anyone who will listen, is that teaching online is a lot of work, and it is hard work, but then I think teaching is hard work anyway.
>
> —Kathleen O'Connell

In this chapter we explore how teachers and students construct worthwhile learning experiences by developing a social, cognitive, and teaching presence. Learners are encouraged to form meaningful connections and contribute to and sustain a rich discourse. The teacher facilitates these connections and discussions by interacting with the students through reflection, synthesis, and feedback.

PRESENCE IN STUDENT-CENTERED ONLINE COURSES

Having presence in the online classroom refers to both the students and the teacher. As teachers online, we must ask ourselves how to balance our presence and our students' presence in a student-centered classroom. Do we work to make students' voices equal to ours, or should students even take priority (and, if so, how can we make this happen)? In an online course, we don't limit our presence to when we interact with each other physically–everyone's presence is understood as unending, fluidly crossing asynchronous and synchronous moments. Without seeing each other, students and instructors recognize that they are all sharing in the journey of the course. Teachers need to authentically know who their students are in order to create course environments that invite students to be present, crafting assignments and discussions that reflect who the students are as learners. Therefore, as teachers, we constantly gather data on how our students are responding to readings and assignments and we modify our teaching to better respond to students' learning needs. We are present for them in this way. The course content and structure must be open to change depending on the class experience.

When teachers commit to understanding what is meaningful for their students they diminish the chances of what Jesse Stommel called the "performance of presence." He suggested that we often privilege the performance of presence over actual presence. We count the number of hours that a student is online and use it as a measure of presence or attendance or learning, when in fact it's simply an agreed-upon role that both teacher and student play to connote being present. He said, "We often require that they have their cameras turned on as though witnessing their attention is more important than their actual attention." Stommel thinks that teachers need to persuade students that their authentic presence, their participation as whole people, is vital to the learning of the whole class.

COUNTERPOINTS

Christopher Bache made the case that every classroom has an invisible psychic field and it's the job of the teacher to channel it and shape it. It's amorphous and it's unscientific but it sort of makes sense, especially now that so many teachers have been teaching online and recognizing that there is a difference in being face-to-face. I think that because of this psychic field—the sum of all of your perceptions of who's paying attention and who's getting it—you can look at students' faces and tell whether something you've just said goes over their heads.
—Howard Rheingold

Integral to supporting student presence is making sure students know that faculty have a personal stake in their learning. This personal stake can manifest in several ways. Students want to know that the instructor is present, pays attention, and cares deeply about their learning needs for academic success. They need to know that they are seen and welcome as who they are. Jessica Blum-DeStefano, faculty in the Progressive Leadership program at Bank Street Graduate School of Education, explained that her own positionality and identity as an educated "White, cisgender, heterosexual mother with a certain degree of privilege and education" demands that she consciously offer opportunities for students "to enter into spaces and assignments and posts and conversations in ways that best reflect where they are in terms of their identity and their beliefs, and also where they are in the moment." For example, supporting students to offer feedback on the assignment is an opportunity for an exchange rather than the one-way street of professor assigns and student produces. This feedback creates an exchange and a deeper understanding and presence for all in the learning community.

To allow students to develop an authentic presence in online classrooms, the teacher cannot use showing up and submitting papers as sufficient indicators of presence. These do not present the student as a whole person, but as an image on a screen and a collection of assignments. Instead, teachers need to find ways for students to share themselves with the class throughout the course. Students should be able to talk about personal experiences, offer questions about the learning occurring in the classroom, and find moments where their voices resonates as loudly as, if not louder than, the teacher's voice. Students should feel that their own personality and existence are as much a driver of learning in the course as the teacher's.

DESIGNING FOR PRESENCE

Niki Bray, assistant professor of teaching at the University of Memphis, believes that availability and access are fundamental to presence. She appreciates the opportunity that office hours provide for establishing presence. She said that she gives out her cell number and students know they can send her a text 24/7, a privilege that has "never been mistreated, not one time, by a single student. And they've actually been grateful for the access right to me. I let them see my face and hear my voice as much as possible."

Being attentive to student development also defines presence. Bray records a weekly video to recap what the students have completed in the previous week.

> I'll talk about how an idea ties into this week. It's very informal—two or three minutes max. Then, throughout the week, I'm paying attention to their progress. I check every morning to see what's going on. If no one has even attempted a quiz by Wednesday or Thursday, I may send a short video to the whole class and I might say something like, How is everyone? I'm just noticing two people have taken the quiz. So I just want to check in and make sure everything is okay, and if you have any needs, please message me privately. So I reach out to them so they know that I'm on top of it.

Stommel concurs. He believes that the best way for a teacher to assure presence is to know who their students are, to know who they are as educators, and to build the relationship that they want to develop with their students. He remembers being told that a good practice for online teaching is to have a video of yourself introducing weekly expectations at the beginning of every unit in a course, and that this was useful for establishing presence. But he tried this once and found that it was not an approach that was congruent with his teaching style. He explained, "The problem with video, for me, is it puts the teacher at the front of the course. It puts the teacher in this position of being the all-seeing eye in the front of the course. It also privileges and foregrounds my voice, and what I had always tried to do in my teaching was to be working together with my students." Instead, Stommel thought about having a video introduction by a student in the course each week.

> I am finding ways to de-emphasize my own voice, and with online learning, my own face, so students won't just see me. They come into the course and the first thing they see is each other. If you think about how we walk into physical

> classrooms, we walk in and we see a room of people. How do we create an online course so the first thing we see is a room full of people?

Similarly, Chris Friend feels that online courses offering an intro video of a talking head, outlining the content of the course and the way it is going to play out, though perhaps well-intentioned, is a bad idea because "that immediately tells students they are working with a premanufactured course that has nothing to do with who they are and what's going on right then." Friend feels strongly that the introduction to a course always needs to be created in the moment and at the time that class is being offered "because then that lets students know we're speaking to them in real time, offering current connections to their lives."

Video, used purposefully, is a very powerful tool for communicating our intention and humanity. When thinking about her own presence, Blum-DeStefano explained presence this way:

> How do I bring my love for teaching, my love for my students, my belief in the fundamental possibility of this work into the small things of the assignments and the readings I choose, and the ways people contribute and engage, the way I give feedback and just every tiny detail of the course, all the way up to the major assignments?

The biggest shift that Blum-DeStefano made in order to bring this spirit and intention to her online teaching was using video. "I think it's a place in the course where I think my voice and authorship stand the strongest because I have to make decisions about every single part of that work. And then we engage in discussion around the video. Using video replaces the part of class on-ground, where I would share some stories and metaphors and examples and an interactive lecture."

Blum-DeStefano gave a lot of thought to the purpose of using video to address her presence. She explained that in her online meetings, especially when students were muting, she was not getting the same level of energy and was concerned about how content was landing. "And so I decided to distill the key things that I would say about a topic for a week, a story I like to share, and build it into a video that could also be responsive

> **TIPS**
>
> I think some of it is a mental block; the technology creates anxiety for folks and it feels harder to troubleshoot and problem solve in the moment. If something goes awry technology-wise, I feel that, even though I consider myself very tech-savvy, if there's a glitch, I feel myself panic. It's probably just a matter of getting more comfortable as I teach online. I think I would get better at figuring out solutions on the spot, and so I think some of it is just giving myself time. —Soyoung Park

to what had been happening in the current iteration of the class." Blum-DeStefano used video to communicate her presence so her students could see her modeling her own subjectivity. Using video has become integral to her online teaching practice. She commented further,

> It felt really scary to do at first and silly because I'm not a YouTuber, but this has been a place where I have thought a lot about the craft and what kinds of things need to happen synchronously. What kinds of things can we move to an asynchronous space to save room for other kinds of learning when we're together? And I felt like those out-loud sharing parts of a course when you're the teacher was the key thing I needed to move away from. Why is everybody here? To listen to me talk? I can do that in another way. So I guess that would be one example of something central to defining my presence.

Blum-DeStefano asserted that using video was crucial for her own growth and development as a teacher. She was afraid that the joy she felt in teaching would be lost in the move online, but found "it taps into that same spirit if you allow it to."

As we examine our own presence and create experiences that support and deepen the presence of our students, it is also essential to examine how presence can contribute to equity. Howard Rheingold addresses this idea by the simple way he refers to his students as "esteemed co-learners." And with that simple turn of a phrase he makes clear to the student that "we're going to try to do things in a different way and I'm going to diminish a little bit of my teacher power and you're going to increase a little bit of you taking responsibility for your learning." Rheingold also addresses his own presence by recognizing that the teacher "has to be much more of a participant online than in a face-to-face class. The teacher must get involved in the conversation and not just give a grade at the end of the quarter." He acknowledges that it's more work because the teacher needs to find something useful to say in response to students. And that creates an engaging presence for both the teacher and students.

Cali Morrison strongly believes that the thing that kills presence is structuring discussions by requiring a certain number of posts or a certain number of words. She said,

> You can have those asynchronous conversations that can be robust, but they have to be nurtured. And part of this nurturing requires us to provide our own robust responses to students. They notice if you don't. Online teaching pulls in students who may have been sitting in the back row who never raise their hands to speak. These asynchronous conversations allow the quieter students to have a voice in a different way. When people are making their otherwise silent voices, thoughts, and learning evident, this contributes to a richer and more equitable presence.

Chris Friend considers presence in an online class to be successful when "concepts from the course are still present in the minds of the students when they are not thinking of themselves as attending a class." He clarified that he feels his presence most when he begins to learn about the subject matter from students who have brought in outside resources or applied their perspectives to the content. When students have inspired him to rethink what he thought he already knew, or offered him a new and interesting way to apply knowledge, he feels his presence as well as his students' presence. Friend explained that as students become intentional contributors of resources, it shows a desire to be responsible for their learning. He said, "I'm responding to my students, not the content. To me, that's presence in an online class."

Quotables

Working with technologies can lead to a certain kind of awkwardness, which isn't terrible but probably makes students impatient. "Why is she doing that?" It's clumsy. It's not smooth. We all like to be smooth. We've all seen ourselves have our moments of success, where one thing led to another but this feels like going back to square one, maybe square three.
—Helen Freidus

In online learning, it is important to shift attention from the teacher, who's no longer at the front of the classroom, to the classroom community. Teachers need to be more attentive to their students, shifting the attention of the class to the things that they contribute to the learning experience. Teachers also need to find ways to make clear for the students what it means to have an authentic presence in the online classroom. It's not enough to simply upload a video of a talking head. Instead, the teacher needs to bring their own sense of self and humanity to the learning environment and model what that looks like for the students. They need to help students understand what it means to be truly involved and that their involvement is essential to knowledge-building and understanding.

REDEFINING TEACHER PRESENCE

Jeremy Knox feels that it is essential to think critically and creatively about what it means for the teacher to be present. He believes that it is problematic to think that the presence of the teacher can only be offered synchronously, emulating the experience of being present that's taken for granted in the physical classroom. He explained that it is helpful to think about teaching online as the teacher and student being embodied in the design of the course and assessments. The presence of the teacher is connected to how the learning environment is structured. Knox has argued that presence is productive when there are points where teachers can see that students are present by their engagement. They might not hear students' voices, but they can see that students have responded and students can see that the teacher has commented or given feedback. Students can acknowledge when someone is paying attention to what they are doing. Knox believes these ideas build a more complex idea of what it means for teachers and their students to be present.

An idea Jesse Stommel has adopted into his teaching practice is the recognition of just how complex students are and how complex their lives are and "how important it is for us to ask them how they're doing. Start a Zoom session with 'Hello, how are you?' Acknowledge that actual human beings will show up to the course and that the core of the course is not just a stack of content." Stommel emphasizes the necessity of extending our humanity to the students. For example, how do we respond to a student who took a long time to figure out how to log on? Do we dismiss that student or do we reach out and ask what we can do to support the student? This question is a good example of how a teacher can extend their humanity to students at any level. While teachers may think that technology issues are none of their concern, instead of suggesting the student call the help desk, they could instead empathize with the student and discuss how they have resolved similar issues in the past. Or they could invite other students to share if they have encountered this problem and share ideas for solutions. Of course, the help desk may also be a solution, but any response should be seen as another way to be present for the students, not a chance to shift the responsibility for a problem.

Blum-DeStefano feels strongly that students need to know that our first priority as teachers is to make sure they are okay, that they are safe and able to engage in the class community. She reaches out with intention. If a student does not show up for class, instead of immediately explaining that they are in danger of failing the class, she provides them with a plan for catching up. But first and most importantly, she wants to know people are okay. She explained,

> When you think about the universes of people that we intersect with, even just in our small community, there's a good chance that someone is hurting deeply at any moment. I would say to the student that ours is a class about supporting adult development. You are more important than a checklist. You are more important than a particular due date. If you feel trusted and valued and believed in, as a student, by your teacher, you feel more accountable to the work, right? I think the simple act of believing in someone inspires good work. And if the work can't happen it is not necessarily a statement about me as a teacher or a reflection of them as learners. It's usually just a byproduct of circumstance. The arc of our relationship extends far beyond a course. And so whatever a student needs, I will just continue to be present.

Rena Palloff said that she began teaching online pretty hands-off in the online environment, tossing it completely to the students and letting them engage with one another on the discussion board. "This was at the beginning when we didn't have great technologies to work with. I would jump in strategically when I felt I needed to support the conversation going on asynchronously. But students would often say they didn't get enough of me." At first Palloff wasn't sure what was going on but then thought to herself that she wanted to experiment with this feedback, and in doing so, deepened her understanding of presence in an online environment. She said,

> The increased availability of good synchronous technologies and the ability to record—because for a long time trying to record something and put it in a course was absolutely impossible—all of these technological advances have worked to my advantage in terms of being able to increase my instructor presence. My colleagues who developed and continue to promote the *Community of Inquiry Framework* [Garrison et al., 2007] talk about three forms of presence that I always focus on: Social (I want people to connect); Community (I want to create a community); and Interaction (I want interaction among students). However, I'm also part of that community, so my presence needs to be noted in some way. So I've become more comfortable over the years with exercising a bit of teaching presence, rather than just letting the content that I've put together do that. I've taken more ownership of my own presence.

Taking ownership of one's presence doesn't have to be large. It can start by being more attentive to the variety of needs that students have. Teacher presence can be found in something as small as the question, How are you doing?

Julie Coltharp, dean of online programs and of faculty development at Ozarks Technical Community College in Missouri, adds that presence includes the capacity and willingness to reflect on our own practice and be willing to grow. She currently runs a center for faculty development and when she hears faculty share their concerns about students who don't do the readings or follow

For Your Consideration

Going back to that idea of presence, how much do you actually have to see a person in order to feel a sense of presence? I think about synchronous versus asynchronous and I think synchronous is really powerful but I don't think you need very much of it. For example, when you meet up with colleagues at a yearly academic conference and then spend the rest of the year engaging with those people asynchronously and at a distance, you do just fine. And the next time we see these colleagues we feel close and we feel connected. —Jesse Stommel instructions for the assignments, she believes that putting faculty in the role of the learner is a real eye-opener for some. She said,

> You need to ask yourself, Why am I including this in my course? You have to make sure it serves a purpose because students can go to the Internet to get so much information. So what value does this reading or assignment add? What's your experience with this assignment? What makes it special? What can they only get from you? So I think really bringing yourself into the classroom and being able to share your own experiences and help them connect the dots is essential. This is the content, but here's why you need to know this. Here's how you can apply this in your world now and move forward. So it's connecting the dots, bringing your authentic self into the classroom, and getting your students to follow suit as well.

Genevieve Lowry, faculty in the Child Life Online program at Bank Street Graduate School of Education, consistently communicates with her students through video. "I will often just make one if something comes to me from a post, and I want all of my students to note it. I make a quick video and send it out as I'm reading the discussions and share how reading this makes me think about a story." Lowry also makes intro and wrap-up videos that pull together the themes, sharing what's coming up the following week and what her expectations are. She explained,

> I also think making videos gives students a way to know me. Going online created an openness that I didn't have in the structure of a two-hour time slot. In my medical aspects class, I created videos called "Child Life Tips." And they're grounded in whatever the topic is that week. In a Child Life Tip on Developmental Interaction, I'll explain what a developmental interaction is and I'll give examples and I'll show things that I've used in my own practice. I explain things developmentally and I use an analogy to do that to scaffold learning. There's one for almost every single week in the medical aspects class, such as keeping families connected when they're isolated in isolation rooms. Students love these because they are specific, content-driven tips.

Blum-DeStefano adds to this, discussing how important it is to be intentional and purposeful in defining one's presence. She said that all the ways in which we engage with students define our presence.

> I think the big thing about presence is recognizing that it means different things to different people. I think a lot about my own presence and how my style—and all the things I do as a way of expressing myself—land differently for different people. I really try to be very intentional about meeting people where they are while also sharing my presence as an expression of myself. So, the way that I

respond on the discussion board, the way that I frame my emails, the way that I write feedback are all huge pieces for presence. And that is a place where you can get very up close and personal with students and their work.

Her presence often comes through the feedback she gives students on their work. They often tell her that when they read her comments, they can hear her voice. Blum-DeStefano said that her goal is to make sure all of her students experience that presence.

Anna Divinsky, artist and assistant professor at Penn State University, also talked about how important it is for students to know that professors are always available and accessible. She explained, "Sometimes there are students who do not respond to emails or submit their assignments. I reach out to them individually and say, 'I noticed that you didn't submit your work. I hope you're okay. What can I do to support you? Let's work out a plan to move forward and help you succeed in the course.'" This attention is especially important at the beginning of the course so there is time for the student to catch up and to know that the professor is being attentive. Divinsky also thinks that asking for feedback at various times throughout the course lets students know that the professor cares about how the course is going for the students. She is interested in everyone's perspective and voice. Divinsky believes that reaching out to the students and encouraging them to be in touch is an important way to bring presence into a course. She believes teachers should share their stories so that students know who they are and where they come from. "I think sharing personal narratives encourages students to be open, making them feel heard, included, and supported. Inviting them to tell their stories and acknowledging their experiences is very important. I remind the graduate instructors that

Counterpoints

What I miss about having a physical presence is the opportunity to build stronger relationships with students. The student who comes to class early. The student who hangs out after class to ask questions. The one who is going to clean up the classroom afterward. We have an informal conversation about this or that, the things that make us feel human. We're all very professional in our roles and we can still laugh at ourselves on Zoom and everything, but just to have those face-to-face conversations is something I miss. I'm always looking for good students to take more classes with me and be a mentor to them. I'm always looking for women, in particular, to take my coding classes. I feel that I'm missing out on mentorship opportunities. I want to know what my students are doing and where they're applying for their internships and their jobs and that's a little bit harder online. —Kristen Sosulski it is crucial that we listen to what the students are telling us and convey to them that we are here for them." Divinsky is mindful of what she says and how she says it online. Providing students with feedback, both oral and written, engages them in learning and creates presence for everyone in the community.

INVITING STUDENT PRESENCE

Shireen Soliman, artist and educator at Parsons School of Design and at Pratt Institute, addresses the way we can humanize the online experience by simply taking the time to be present with one another. "Imagine if we bumped into each other on the elevator on the way to class, what would we talk about on the way up?" Soliman talked about how she offers the opportunity for everyone to be present with one another before focusing on the course content.

> We do some breathing exercises, some chair yoga. We create class lists, like a class playlist of our favorite music or our favorite places around school that we missed during the pandemic. We create a little review so that we can know where the great coffee spots are. Trying to stimulate conversation to de-escalate the anxiety, the exhaustion from not sleeping, the panic from watching the news all day, to just get ourselves in a space where we're receptive to being in this moment to learn.

Negar Farakish shared an idea that she learned from a colleague, Todd Cherches, adjunct assistant professor at NYU's School of Professional Studies and author of *VisuaLeadership*. Cherches talks about three Vs: visibility, voice, and value (Cherches, 2020). Farakish explained that visibility is knowing if we are being seen and how we are being seen. Voice asks if our voices are being heard and how they are being heard. And the third V asks what is the value we are getting from and adding to the class. Farakish said,

> So I borrowed that concept from Todd and I have created some slides around it for the first session of the class. There's one slide when there are different presences on Zoom: somebody just has a name, somebody has a picture, somebody has a video on but is on a cellphone. Somebody looks bored. And then there is somebody who's looking right at the camera, is dressed appropriately, and the picture is clear and focused. And I asked students, Which one do you want to be? This is how you are going to be seen. You're going to be visible, but you have a lot of options for how you are going to be visible. Then we talk about voice and I tell them that I can hear their voices in many ways: raise your hand and talk, put your voice in the chat. When you are in your breakout rooms and you're working on your discussion questions and you're putting notes into the

Google doc, I hear you there. Then we get to the issue of value—getting and contributing value.

Farakish said that students know they are expected to make a comment, but she distinguishes for students the difference between making a comment and making a comment that contributes value. "And I can tell you that every time I go through this, I've set the tone and expectations very clearly. I expect everybody to contribute and we want to make sure we hear from everybody." Demonstrating for the students how to recognize how their contributions bring value to the learning community makes the community that much more authentic, according to Farakish.

Along with the teacher providing strategies for what it means to be present, Blum-DeStefano shared some considerations for thinking about the technical aspect of presence online. She thinks it's important to have cameras on, but she added, "I think just trusting people is important. If you can have your camera on, I trust you will have your camera on." She added that she appreciates students leaving their microphones on because that lends itself to a more authentic version of noise. "But if you're in a space where you have a barking dog, a crying baby, a roommate who's in a class behind you, of course, turn your microphone off." She said that letting people know that the space of being together is important to everyone is essential. "Everyone's presence matters and I trust students are present, even if they're not visible." She acknowledged that teachers can't confirm the presence of a student whose camera is off, but "I think if we lead with the assumption that people are doing their best, it removes a barrier that would otherwise be there between the instructor and the student."

For Your Consideration

If I go back to when I started teaching online, back in like 2003, my presence was all text-based. I was using Blackboard and it was just announcements at the time. And then I remember after a few years just making one change and I was still doing my announcements, but in my announcements, I would record them using an audio tool called Audacity. I would produce an MP3 and I would upload it. And I'd tell my students to listen or read. "You have your choice," because that accessibility piece was always there and universal design for learning has always informed me. And the connections with my students were so much deeper and I can remember one time I had a cold and they could hear my stuffy nose in my audio announcement. And I received messages from my students like, "Oh, I'm so sorry. You're not feeling well. I hope you're feeling better this week." And

I thought, well, that's really interesting. And then I was sitting at graduation and I remember hearing the name of one of my online students get called and thinking this is interesting because, you know, after the ceremony, there's that time when the faculty would hug their students and high-five their students. And I'm like, I don't know what my students look like and they don't know what I look like. And then I started trying to figure out how to use video, and video back then was hard. YouTube was starting to emerge. But that was another reason why I wanted to use VoiceThread even though I wasn't using YouTube yet: I was able to record a video of myself using VoiceThread and they could see me. And then I can remember parking my car in the parking lot at school and getting out of my car and a student coming up to me and saying, "You're my online instructor." And I thought, "Oh my gosh, this is it," right? We need to bridge the online classroom with the real world and those connections were super powerful in my mind.—Michelle Pacansky-Brock

Whether a teacher setting standards for what it means to have a visible presence online in a literal sense, meaning the camera is on, or visible in an engaged sense, meaning the camera may be off or the speaker may be muted, Soliman makes clear that all teachers should be considerate of how the students want to be present with regard to camera presence. She explained her compact with the students:

> One of the things that we agree with is that, at the very least, when each of us is speaking about our work, we're going to turn the camera on, even if it's for two minutes. I'm presenting my work, and I'm going to connect with you and have that non-verbal and verbal communication. So the camera doesn't have to be on 100% of the time. Fatigue is real, the exhaustion is real, but we find a balance and I think people appreciate that balance. It's very hard for me, of course, to talk to a group of black screens. But I think that we have a mutual appreciation for each other, and we have that understanding. So I know that the black screens aren't going to last throughout the class.

Soliman also spoke about seeking affirmation of understanding.

> Let me get a thumbs-up if you can't come on the screen. You need to give me the emoji reaction. So they have options through chat or emojis or verbally. I think people like options and those options don't exist on-ground. When we're face-to-face, if I ask for understanding, the only option is verbal. I guess they could nod their heads, but sending me a private note in the chat is not available on-ground. So this is another way that students can be quiet but their presence is still felt.

From the beginning, as Amy Lewis found her way into online classrooms, she wondered what would happen to her presence. As a program coordinator for 100 students in an elementary education program, Lewis works hard to know each of her students. She explained, "If I'm telling my students to get to know their students, then that has to be part of the work I do online." In all of the courses she teaches, she does identity work in which students fill out surveys and compose narratives about who they are, and she considers how to critically connect all of this to the subject matter. She thinks about how to use what she is learning about her students to demonstrate that she cares and knows about them as learners, and to make that knowledge and caring visible through class discussion. Lewis believes that demonstrating a commitment to knowing her students as learners will influence them to know their students as learners, "and if we don't do that, our students feel it."

TIPS

Using a message board—well it can't be just any message board. They have to have certain characteristics and just using a message board is not going to work unless you know how to do it. For example, I would start out with just a minimum number of threads: One about what we're doing here, one to ask questions, another one to introduce ourselves. And another one about "What should we talk about here?" and from "What should we talk about here?" we would break out threads. It wasn't uncontrolled, it was slowly building.
—Howard Rheingold

Soyoung Park, faculty member and director of programs in early childhood special education at Bank Street Graduate School of Education, believes that in the online experience, keeping the prompts simple, making the task itself simple, and not overwhelming the students has been really critical for presence in discussions. She said,

> Students will be engaged in a discussion and you'll have some who are invested, present, and want to share a lot. You'll also have others who simply answered the question. And so I think the simplicity of the prompt or the task allows for more than one way of being present. So if you are the kind of person who wants to go in and just do the bare minimum, then you can do that. If you're the person who wants to go in and post, and then read everyone else's responses and respond to others, you can do that, too.

Park believes that students do see thoughtfulness and intentionality in how a teacher may curate an online class. She explained,

> I find where the moments of transition are, where I can pull out important themes that came up in the discussion and then build on them and share that

> insight. When I'm in the breakout rooms, I take notes furiously on just what are the things that are coming up in these conversations, and when we come back together, I can then highlight a few of the things that came out and then add whatever it is that I feel like I need to add. And so I think that's where my voice and presence are strong.

Kristen Sosulski spends a lot of time thinking about course design separate from her actual teaching. And the one thing she treasures about this process is how she created access for students to be present. She explicitly uses words that represent a call to action on the part of the students.

> I use verbs to illustrate things that represent student actions in the class. For example, "join" as in "join the Zoom meeting." I also use words such as "read, engage, and practice." I use these verbs as a call to action. It's a small part of the design, but I really cherish it because it reminds me to put the student at the center of the learning. Whether they're engaging with each other in online conversations or they are focused on practicing different problem sets and things that I give them, I really get excited about curating what students are going to do.

Sosulski clearly described her optimistic approach to online teaching. "If you design for it, it will happen." She shared an example of something we've all experienced: We ask a question and only one person answers. "If you're just getting the first person who speaks up to answer the question, then you're excluding others and you're creating a pattern in your class that the first person answers the question and then the conversation moves on." She also thinks another way to encourage student presence is to let students know when something they've posted is especially important for learning and ask if they would start the next class by sharing their thinking from the post. This is one way that Sosulski encourages and enhances student presence.

Faculty presence has a significant impact on encouraging students to be known and sensed. Cheri Gurse finds presence inspiring when there is

> **QUOTABLES**
>
> One thing that is very clear is that good teaching is good teaching. I always use this analogy. I don't know how to cook but my husband has a passion for cooking. If you come to my house, the kitchen looks like a culinary laboratory. All kinds of gadgets, all kinds of state-of-the-art tools. But when I go there, they're useless to me. So that's the analogy that I use in terms of different platforms and online technologies. If you don't know the principles of good teaching, you can have all the tools and resources available to you but they're just tools. —Negar Farakish

a back-and-forth written exchange between her and the student in response to an assignment. "I ask students to respond to two or three of my comments on their paper in ways that will expand their thinking. Choose the ones that turn you on—where will you learn the most?" As Gurse responds to her students' responses, a thoughtful exchange evolves. When giving feedback, teachers can be engaged with their students' thinking and learning, and often the teacher is engaged as a learner as well. Asking questions and genuinely leaning into the work with curiosity and enthusiasm will support a student in experiencing the instructor's presence.

Taking the time to share who we are in a way that reflects our humanity and invites students to share who they are is an important step to bringing presence into our online classrooms. Presence in online teaching and learning can be a great equalizer between teacher and student. By developing a community and classroom experience that builds on the personal and academic interests of the students while also providing those students with the tools and resources to understand the value of their voices, teachers effectively create more balanced and active environments. With the online space, teacher presence no longer has to be defined as simply the teacher teaching in front of and to the students. Instead, by designing courses sensitively, asking questions that are meaningful to all facets of a student's learning, and acting as a partner in both learning and inquiring, teachers give each student more opportunities to bring their voices to the learning community, and can also move away from the center of the course. In this more communal experience, knowledge and thought are shared and ever-changing based on student engagement and responsiveness to the learning goals of the entire community. There are myriad options for students to be heard and myriad options for teachers to have their presence felt and their voices heard. As we continue to examine and advance our online pedagogy, considering our presence and how it impacts our teaching and our learning, as well as that of our students, is essential for developing a strong and inclusive pedagogy for teaching online.

Ask Yourself

How do you make room for getting to know your students and for them to know you?

In developing your online course, how do you design for the ever-changing world in which your students live?

Does your design allow for you to shift gears if a student has an idea that enhances the learning?

CHAPTER 5

Communities

> The thing I've learned about building online classes is: Never do it alone.
>
> —Clay Shirky

In this chapter we explore the potential of the online classroom as a learning community where all learners contribute to inquiry, knowledge, and expertise. These contributions inform and deepen the understanding of what is taught in the course. The digital space also provides a unique opportunity for learners to expand the knowledge within the community by accessing resources and expertise generated by other communities and sharing that knowledge.

ONLINE CLASSROOM COMMUNITIES

Understanding the online classroom as a community is central to it being a successful learning experience for teachers and students. Learning is a social activity and we learn best when we learn from each other, negotiating ideas and engaging in a shared discourse. In a learning community, students build knowledge together. The contributions of the whole inform and deepen the understanding of the ideas and concepts being taught. Communities provide norms to guide how the members can learn from each other and feel safe to take risks. The practitioners we interviewed describe this aspect of online teaching and learning as central to all other aspects of the online experience. In order for engagement, inquiry, equity, and presence to develop and strengthen, students and teachers need authentic connections, belonging, and interdependence. To establish their classrooms as communities, some teachers brought their on-ground teaching experience online, replicating community-building activities and translating them for the digital space. Some teachers believe that building a community online is more work, and some believe it is a different kind of work. However, all practitioners agreed that building learning communities online needs to be intentional; since interactions among students and teachers are mediated and at a distance, teachers teaching in digital spaces cannot take it for granted that communities will develop. Online teaching and learning has been falsely represented as students studying alone with no interaction among classmates, learning in isolation instead of together as a community. However, as teachers become more conscious of the need for the purposeful development of communities for learning online, they have also begun to reflect on the interactions of their students in their on-ground courses, questioning whether community development is automatic just because the students are together in a physical space. In this chapter, we look at how teachers have approached the building of community in their online courses and what they learned from and with the communities they have built.

> **TIPS**
>
> If you're in an online class and your students aren't participating, I think, "Don't hate the modality." You reflect and see what you're doing and try something else because it's really on you as the faculty to make that course engaging, to get them to want to respond and participate and build connections and grow. You're not just dumping content on them; you're facilitating conversations and you're trying to engage them and get them to connect with that content and make it valuable for them. —Julie Coltharp

Experienced teachers new to teaching online may have doubts about building authentic learning communities online. Merle Keitel, chair of the division of Psychological and Educational Services and professor of counseling psychology at Fordham University's Graduate School of Education, describes how her practice is dependent on connecting with the students to encourage a sense of community. As she started teaching online, Keitel wondered how her emotional self would translate online and whether she would be able to engage her students without being physically in the room. She then found that her ability to connect with the students emotionally became more prominent, central, and intentional online. Keitel explained,

> I found that I could encourage community by communicating my own personal caring for students—the pandemic and the isolation, the death, and all of what my students were going through, the division, the racial divides, the tensions in our country were all so strong. To me there was never a more important time to keep a sense of community and provide a space for support and exchange of ideas in a trusting and safe environment. So that was a primary goal for me in teaching online, that the students felt that they could connect on a human level with others and be part of a community. And that happens by communicating, caring, checking in with students, making sure that they're okay, making sure they know they can email me and set up appointments outside of class if they need additional support. I think that it worked well, and that was the feedback that I got from students.

Many teachers are concerned that their class community is dependent on the interactions defined by physical space. When redesigning her course to be taught online, Shireen Soliman had to consider how to reproduce the supportive community that is formed by the teacher and students in an art studio. The community that develops in Soliman's on-ground course was connected to the possibilities of the physical art studio where students share their work and teacher and students provide feedback within the space where the art is conceived of and created. She wanted to reproduce this fluid and engaged environment online and looked for technologies that gave everyone the ability to share work with the group collaboratively and where they could see the works next to each other as a whole. She needed to create an online format where it would be easy for everyone involved to give feedback and for students to experience the dynamics of artists interacting in a studio. Soliman ended up recreating the studio experience online using a Miro or Mural whiteboard, which brought some unexpected benefits that she and her students appreciated. They found that sharing artwork was easy and convenient. The use of digital whiteboards opened multiple pathways for sharing feedback, made engagement and interaction visible, and it enabled the permanence of the shared work as a whole. Soliman explained,

> There was this component in my on-ground course where we were putting the work on the wall and we would stand back to see the whole studio's work. And so how do we replicate that online? Digital, collaborative whiteboard spaces allowed us to see and share work, in a format different from printing, not seeing it eye level on a wall but seeing it in the digital space. Everybody is uploading quickly, dragging and dropping, there is no learning curve. They are able to grab a post-it note. They are able to give immediate feedback to one another. They are able to benefit from seeing the whole group's work. They are able to grab emojis. They need to be able to communicate in so many ways, so many levels. So during the class, we are talking verbally, but they are also getting different levels of feedback that way. I think that the collaborative whiteboard space for me was critical to being able to continue that engagement, to know that they are engaged and that they are giving each other feedback. They love it. They don't want to have one more heavy lift. They want to grab a post-it note and just start typing. It just needs to feel intuitive, and in the whiteboard space, every cursor is assigned a name. You get to see these different cursors appear. So you see everyone in this space. It's the same thing in the collaborative, digital whiteboard. You get to see everybody's cursor. You see the frenetic movement of everybody going around looking at work and all the cursors jumping over to go look at a specific work. And so you are seeing everyone is engaged.

Soliman found that the online classroom offered exciting opportunities for all of her students to engage and connect, which served to strengthen the community. Building a community is not dependent on in-person interaction in the physical space; instead, as these and other practitioners describe, it is connected to establishing authentic, dynamic, and emotional spaces for teaching and learning.

For Your Consideration

One of the things I want to say about instructional design is that I've been an instructional designer, both in corporate and educational spaces, and I always try to break the rules in the interest of integrating a more critical pedagogical approach. My experience with instructional designers is that most of them are very earnest about wanting to help both faculty and students in a learning situation. They are as much teachers as the rest of us. However, they are constrained by expectations from the university for what their job is and what they're supposed to be producing.
—Sean Michael Morris

GETTING TO KNOW THE STUDENTS

In order to build community, students need to know one another and feel a sense of belonging in the course community. Most teachers highlight that this has to happen at the beginning of the class experience as it prepares everyone for how to engage in the course. Rena Palloff uses the beginning of the course for her and her students to know each other, to feel welcome, and to make the expectation of community explicit.

> To create community, and it really helps to kick things off, I have a course orientation on Zoom. I invite everybody to a Zoom session where I walk them through the course. "This is how we're going to do this, these are my expectations, this is what I expect from you, this is what you can expect from me." We take our time just getting to know each other and getting used to each other and I have them do introductions: "This is who I am and what I do, but this is also my learning style." This is how I engage them so that they start to learn more about each other, and I have found that to be a particularly effective technique. I also ask them to post something about themselves that they didn't mention in their introductions so that they can go a little deeper and start welcoming each other in. I do that right away. That's week one and then we can start working in class. I don't touch the content until we've had an opportunity to get to know each other.

Similarly, to help her students feel they belong, Cheri Gurse starts each online class with a poll, or multiple polls. She asks a series of questions: How are you feeling right now? What are you concerned about? Are you concerned or worried? What is on your mind right now? This is a structured way of inviting students in that Gurse designed specifically for teaching online. She explained, "That's nothing that I ever did in person. I just maybe turned on music or maybe we chit-chatted and all that, but this became official and structured in my online teaching. And what it does in the classroom is it models this process of dialogue and inquiry."

For Detra Price-Dennis, what really mattered is how to immerse students in the course. "Do they feel like this is something that they're clicking through or do they feel like this is something they're a part of? And then what are the ways that they can collaborate when they're in that space and grow their thinking together?" Price-Dennis finds that in online courses the community needs to be intentionally built. She starts by asking students, "What do you need as a learner in this class?" She brainstorms with the students and creates a set of class intentions based on what students have stated that they need as learners. They then make an intention chart or visual that Price-Dennis puts on the homepage of each course, and students return to the list throughout the course. This list is different for each class. Price-Dennis explains that this is a way of being intentional about creating community online. "It's really being proactive. Asking people upfront, What do you need? It's really starting there, not trying to figure it out after." She also has a structure for helping students to be aware of and connected to their intentions and ideas through visuals and ongoing reflection.

> **COUNTERPOINTS**
>
> Just having people together in a room online does not automatically create community the same way that it might on the ground, because empathy is easier to build when we see people in three dimensions. Empathy is easier to build when someone can't just turn the camera off and disappear from our sight. When I know that I'm going to click a Leave Meeting button that ends our interaction, there's less need for an investment. —Chris Friend

> I have them do an assignment that in some classes is called an ideation board and some call a multimodal notebook. But the point of it is to trace your own thinking and ideas throughout the class. And then how do those show up at a final assignment? The point is that you are using that ideation board for the whole class to try to figure out "What do I care about? What is important to me? What questions do I have? What do I need to read? What conversations do I need to have in this class? Who do I need to talk to?" And it is visual, it is multimodal, it is going through the steps to try to figure out an answer to a problem. And then they share what they learned in the end, in the form of some *thing*, so that inquiry is built in from the very first class and who we are as learners and as a community. And the questions we have sit alongside the content of the class.

CREATING OPPORTUNITIES FOR COMMUNITY INTERACTION

The online classroom, with its flexible structure, can provide different ways for students to interact, giving them choices for how they want to communicate with one another, helping them to be included in the class community. These interactions may be synchronous or asynchronous, whole group, small group, or one-on-one. They may be posted to the forum as written text or recorded video. Soliman emphasizes the importance of creating different opportunities for students to interact with one another in her course. She engages students in small breakout rooms, whole group discussions, and individual activities. She creates different levels of interaction depending on student needs. Soliman explained, "If a student is less comfortable in the whole group, I give them the opportunity in a smaller group, something more intimate, being able to have access to just me. For some students, that is important. And so all of that starts to build and establishes that culture of community and safety."

Some teachers find that building a community is easier than in the physical classroom. They highlight that students tend to use the same well-worn pathways to connect with their classmates as they do in in-person classes. They find the people they know or those with whom they find comfort, and stay with them. With online teaching, especially with synchronous technologies, there is more of an opportunity to intentionally cultivate community, where the technology can provide options that may not be available in the traditional classroom, such as the ability to pair students randomly (breakout rooms) or to survey students to form study groups around commonalities or differences (polling). Shelley Vermilya, an artist-educator who teaches gender studies at Saint Michael's College in Vermont, highlights the power of breakout rooms, noting that what she loves about that feature of synchronous teaching is that she can ensure how the students are "not in the same little cluster that they make the first day of class and never break out of."

Tips

The class that I'm most proud of is an instructional design class that I developed as a faculty at Manhattan College in collaboration with LaSalle University in Colombia. We went abroad and we met some faculty in the School of Education and they wanted to partner with us. And I said, "Well, why don't we start partnering on a class?" So we designed this class, and it was great. The students had to interact with each other and learn about cultural biases and differences and how to work with each other through technology and that was amazing. And then they had to actually use technology in their final project to solve a problem. And that, for me, was the best class I ever designed because it was collaborative; it was a problem solver; and the technology was not a hindrance. Technology became a catalyst for creative thinking. Did I know that was going to happen? Not really, but after it started to come together, it was phenomenal. And that course has led to 10 articles and presentations because two countries collaborating with students to produce one product, you would think wouldn't be novel, but it was novel. —Shawna Bu Shell

An essential requirement for building community is for the teacher to support students in understanding that their learning is not isolated but dependent on the learning of others in their classroom. Teachers can take different approaches to cultivate this understanding. Chris Friend responds to course discussions by communicating to the whole class, demonstrating to the students that they are learning together as a community. He participates in the class conversation by responding holistically to the discussion instead of responding directly to individual posts. He uploads his responses as videos and pins them to the top of the forum page. He explained,

> I will say, "Here's the nature of the conversation that I have seen happening so far. Here's what I think our class is discussing. Here are the trends that I've noticed that seem to be emerging from what we've been saying. And here are some highlights." So, for instance, this one post is a really great example of how this should be done, and if you're struggling with this go check out so-and-so's post because they did a really good job with it. Or check out so-and-so's reply to that other person because their reply highlighted a challenge that the first person struggled with and gave them a great suggestion for a way to recover from it and the first person is going to be better off now that another person has contributed to this discussion. That's the kind of discussion we should be having. And I find that it works really well because if there's a problem developing in the discussion, I can highlight that problem and the students will respond to it and they'll say, "Dr. Friend said in his video that we need to make sure we make this change to what we just read." And they use the pronoun *we* because they recognize that they're all working together to do these things. In an online discussion board, I think saying *we* means a lot. It means that they see themselves working together. This approach teaches the students how to learn with and from each other as members of a learning community in ways that benefit them beyond the class.

For a learning community to develop online, we need to create environments where students are encouraged to learn from each other and to help each other. The students need to understand that each student's accomplishments help to enhance the learning of the community. Palloff shares an example where one of her students had technical difficulties editing a video assignment and another student offered to edit the student's work. She actively supports this kind of collaboration. Palloff explained that we need to create environments where it is okay to act as an expert and to offer help and guidance to one another.

> I think we need to be conscious about creating that community in the online environment. It doesn't just happen, we have to work at it. Being attentive to that and trying to create that sense of community is the first piece, and then, once it happens, to be able to continue to nurture it. It doesn't always work, but this particular example is a beautiful example of when it does work and where people

> are feeling safe and that's really the critical piece, and I try to model that within my classes and encourage that with one another.

QUOTABLES

A common concern by teachers new to teaching online is that they won't be able to build a relationship with their students—although that can be the case with onsite classes as well. This is where I would say it is important to be deliberate about the ways you engage with students and help them find ways to engage with each other.
—Kristen Sosulski

Although community is an essential aspect of online learning, the distance among the students and the mediated status of the digital environment means that students may not immediately understand what community online looks like or how to contribute to the community as a thought leader. The strategies that Friend and Palloff described—modeling for the class what it means to be an engaged community expert, and responding to the work of the class as a collective endeavor—help to clarify for the students the potential of the online space as a community. This may seem odd to some, who think that the students are well prepared to engage in the online classroom as a community, as the social media they are accustomed to are also built on community models. Nonetheless, students may not correlate the digital learning environment to their daily virtual environments. So the role of the teacher as community member, and not just community leader, is important. It helps the students to see how they can contribute to the class community and understand how other students contribute to their learning experience.

GOING BEYOND THE BOUNDARIES OF THE PHYSICAL CLASSROOM

Online learning communities are made up of more than the teachers and students who are listed on the class roster. They also include the professional communities and networks of practitioners linked to the course through the Internet. On the Internet, teachers and students can access resources and bring in experts from various networks to enhance the course experience, finding opportunities for authentic activities and communicating with a multitude of voices to make the classroom more connected to the global community within which the course exists.

Online courses lend themselves to a more in-depth experience with guest speakers. Cheri Gurse requires her students to go online to learn about a guest speaker in advance and come to class prepared with questions. Because of this preparation, her students ask authentic questions as they talk with the speaker. She also encourages her students to go out into the community, asking them to reach out to experts and have conversations with them about their knowledge and interests. Students then share these experiences with the class.

> **COUNTERPOINTS**
>
> It might be a research paper. It could be a video, it could be a blog, it could be a podcast, it could be any number of things. The way that I evaluate this work is through students' self-reflections. They do their own self-evaluations throughout the course twice during the course. I ask them to actually talk about the idea of participation—what participation looks like in an online space, but also specifically for them. So how do you participate? What do you expect of yourself and do you think you're fulfilling that? —Sean Michael Morris

Susie Rolander uses Twitter in her courses to connect students to the larger communities that dwell on the web. She started using Twitter herself after attending a conference and realized she was missing the parallel conversations among attendees that were taking place on social media. The experience of using Twitter and engaging with its massive community was overwhelming for her at first. "I have never had so much professional development in my entire life! I feel like I went from this little person in her own classroom to this huge expanse." Rolander asks her students to use Twitter to find and follow professionals and to build a professional network to learn from and get support. She said,

> One of the things that I tell my students when I talk to them about Twitter is that they have teachers' support throughout their time at the College but there's not really a mode of communication for connecting beyond or outside of the institution. And so I tell them that this is why I want them to use Twitter. I want them to have this network of people that they can have in terms of support, but also to be a part of bigger ideas and movements in education.

Online teachers can invite students to go beyond the classroom and share their ideas with the community found on the web, connecting them with an audience for the work they are producing in class. Friend commented,

> There's something dramatic and magical that happens once a student realizes that something they have created can be linked by someone else out there on the Internet. That completely shifts their sense of self and their sense of audience. It shifts their sense of potential reach. With a traditional class, we may think of a student writing an essay, turning it in on paper. The teacher would read it and return it to the student and the student would throw it in the trash and that was the entire transaction. But instead, if a student writes something and publishes it online, theoretically anyone can find that and index it and document it and refer to it and link to it. They are not writing for the teacher, they are writing

> for the world, and that fundamentally changes our conception of what writing can be and do and where it can exist. And once the students have the experience of writing something or linking to something else they have written and being able to talk about an artifact that they have created as an object of study, that makes their work its own network and it allows them to show connections in ways that the Internet was designed to do.

Using the web to provide public access to student work can help them to make expert connections and build professional relationships. For example, Michelle Pacansky-Brock described an assignment where she encourages students to reach out to photographers:

> I did this really cool project where every student had to find a photographer, anywhere in the world, and contact the photographer, get the photographer to agree to be interviewed, and create a VoiceThread about the photographer's work. It was like a research project. I had them interact and communicate with a real person and the outcomes were pretty wonderful. I had this one student, she submitted her interview project and she said, "Oh my gosh, the photographer wants to know if he can embed my project on his blog." That's just amazing.

It is really important for students to know that the work they do in the classroom is not isolated. Teachers can create authentic experiences by asking students to write for a public audience rather than for the professor. Christina Katopodis's students write for a semi-public audience on Humanities, Arts, Science, and Technology Alliance and Collaboratory (HASTAC), an interdisciplinary community of humanists, artists, social scientists, scientists, and technologists. She explained,

> We created a group on HASTAC called "What we should be writing about right now." Students wrote for a semi-public audience about their local environments, about the past and present history of their neighborhoods and thinking about environmental issues as well as how those issues intersect with social issues such as gentrification. How lower-income neighborhoods are not cared for and that their parks are not as cared for as higher-income neighborhoods. They also write about the land and land ownership. And so students were writing the posts, revising them, making them better in a semi-public frame. Other HASTAC users were commenting on their posts and engaging with them.

Katopodis explained that student focus shifts when there is a real purpose and audience for their writing. Writing with an external audience in mind asks students to be aware of a larger context. As the reader of their writing is not the teacher anymore, students cannot assume the audience has read the books they cite. They need to write about what the authors of the books say and be explicit about their own interpretations.

> How do I talk about Rachel Carson's *Silent Spring* or Ursula K. LeGuin's introduction to *The Left Hand of Darkness* in this public context for people who may not have read these books? When students know that they're engaged with more than just our class, that their work has a life beyond our community, and when they see their work getting attention from a public audience, they feel like they have something valuable to say, that their voices matter and they have some expertise to contribute to the world.

Online communities can go beyond the course by continuing to exist and evolve long after the course has ended. Students who have taken the course before can stay in touch, share information about their practice, and serve as experts or mentors for new students. Amy Lewis sees online teaching and learning as an opportunity to bring a wider community together.

> Because distance isn't an issue when you're meeting remotely, I keep in touch with several of our program completers. I learn about their progress as educators. I have always wanted to have a forum for these practicing teachers to get together to talk about their practice, what they're struggling with, and what they need support with. I see online as an opportunity to do that and to create a network among the students who have graduated and are working, the districts where we conduct a lot of our student teaching, and our current pre-service teachers. So I see the opportunity for a broader network of support.

Online course communities do not need to end, as students can continue to connect long after the scheduled course has finished. Courses can also be structured so students can connect with one another before the class even starts. Indeed, a program can be structured as a learning community for all students studying at the institution. Lin Lipsmeyer shared,

> The online degree program is structured as a cohort. So students are accepted at the same time, they take the same classes, but then they also have their own mentors and each mentor has students from different years and the mentor and students communicate vertically, and they also communicate with previous cohort members. And we also have one week-long meeting each year for all the cohorts and they catch up on things. So we create this community for the students to communicate with their peers, and we also bring speakers. So they have different ways of communicating with both the smaller and larger community.

Whatever approach the community uses to establish itself, it is important that the concept of community permeates the student experience and beyond. Jeremy Knox talked about using his introductory course to instill the values of community. His programs include an icebreaker week at the front of his online courses. Knox has the students do activities that "set them up to get to know each other a little bit before we start the formal course activities."

The introductions may happen in a discussion board, Twitter, Padlet, or using Minecraft. Knox described a recent activity called "Laptop by the Window" where students shared about the physical spaces they were in. While the activities may change, they always include opportunities for everybody to share something about themselves and to get to know each other a little better. "It's fascinating to see all these different spaces that people are studying in. The students really respond to that sense of understanding where other people are coming from. And it's really looking beyond the screen. And you get a real sense of how people are engaging with the program." Knox explained how having program-wide social spaces can be a challenge in graduate programs because after the initial courses they take as a cohort, students take different electives and go in different directions. However, he found that when students create their own social digital spaces on other platforms such as Facebook or Discord, they stay connected to one another.

For Your Consideration

When I took this job, I said, "There will come a day when you don't need a Vice Provost of Educational Technologies any more than you need a Vice Provost for Printed Matter." Schools are going to get good at this. The Internet is going to go away as a special concern. I don't think you can get there in one burst, but my job is to help move the school along to the point where my job doesn't need to exist. —Clay Shirky

The interconnectedness of the digital learning space creates exciting potential for what a classroom community might look like. The concept of the guest speaker is no longer limited to inviting an expert to speak in front of the classroom. Through the web and social media each student has the opportunity to connect to a wide range of people who have experience in the topics being discussed in the class, creating just-in-time guest speakers who can respond to the subjects being discussed by the course, answering questions and addressing ideas presented in the classroom as they happen. Students are also able to showcase their classwork in spaces meant to exhibit ideas and projects for feedback and discussion from communities at large, helping students to experience feedback that goes beyond their immediate peers and teacher.

Course communities can also be extended beyond the traditional structures of the classroom. They may start before the course has begun and may extend well beyond the scheduled end date of the course. There is also the potential for the programs themselves to be structured so that the students within the program are connected to one another during the time they are enrolled in the program. First-year students may be connected to those finishing their programs through central forums and collaborative resources for social and academic purposes. Opportunities to design programs as communities themselves that in turn find pathways for communities outside of the classroom to engage in the learning experience, are endless in an online environment.

COMMUNITIES OF TEACHERS

Online communities are not just for student learning and engagement. Many of the practitioners we interviewed also talked about the importance of being part of a professional community themselves, for designing courses together and for connecting around shared student experiences. Cali Morrison described an online course that was built collaboratively by a group of faculty.

> We had a community where those of us who were teaching the course would get together on a regular basis, about once every other week, to discuss how our students were doing and what tweaks we might need to make to the discussion boards or to the assignments that the students were working on. So the collaborative nature of the community enabled us to improve the experience for the students.

Institutions and conferences are offering more online professional development, which is expanding their reach and making networks of teachers more accessible. Julie Coltharp describes how virtual professional development can be expanded.

> We weren't offering that much virtual PD on our own campus, but now it's the norm. Everything we offer moving forward is going to have a virtual option. I'm also always looking for an academic consortium experience, I'm always looking for opportunities to be a matchmaker. Someone may have a need over here. Or this person's really good at this and so I say, "Let's get you two together. Let's have a conversation."

The connection among faculty of different colleges and universities offers opportunities for teachers to share successes, bringing all types of teachers together to address similar problems of practice, making online teaching and learning stronger.

With online teaching, teachers and students step not into an actual room but into an experience. Instead of a physical space that confines them with one another, their bond is an agreement to connect with each other and to provide support and feedback to everyone involved in the learning. This experience is best understood as a community and it is up to the teacher to help the students understand what it means to be members of an online learning community and to find approaches for encouraging the students to communicate and collaborate with one another while they have committed to learn from each other. The goal of the online teacher is to guide the students by being an exemplary member of the community themselves. They can achieve this standing by presenting themselves as authentic and emotional members of the community, responding to student discussions and activities by acknowledging their efforts as the work of a connected whole, and creating opportunities to engage with members of the community, creating a broad sense of belonging.

If the online classroom is established as a learning community and the students effectively understand that they are a part of that community, as well as multiple communities outside this course, then there are many layers of community that can be explored in the digital space. The teacher can help students navigate and assess the information they are gathering from this larger community, helping them to both better understand their own inquiry and be effective in building deep knowledge.

The teachers may also think outside of the traditional structures of the college classroom, working from the start to build courses that do not subscribe to traditional beginnings and endings, asking students to participate in the community before the start of the learning experience and encouraging them to continue their engagement with one another as learners after the course ends. They may also work with other teachers and administrators to consider extending the community beyond the classroom to the program itself, opening new ways to connect learners at all stages within the program. For example, allowing senior students to strengthen their own knowledge by sharing what they have discovered and how they presented themselves as community members to newcomers looking for advice and mentorship extends the community. And even further afield, teachers may build communities for themselves alongside or around the learning communities they create, examining the practices they are establishing and the experiences they are developing with fellow travelers.

Tips

We start by looking at individual needs and then collectively consider what individual people are saying they need. And then we create the themes. So collectively, this is what we say we need as learners. So then we create a visual. I put it on the front page of every Canvas, because it's different for every class, and we list all the things we need. We're open to feedback. We do whatever it is that people say that they need and want. And we return to that throughout the course. So it's really being proactive, asking people up front: What do you need? It becomes an ideation board and some classes call it a multimodal notebook.
—Detra Price-Dennis

Ask Yourself

In designing your online course, how do you open the door to myriad communities that can influence learning?
What are the communities that make up your online classroom?
How do you support learning from other voices and not just yours?

CHAPTER 6

Time and Space

> What does the future of education look like in all of the different spaces?
>
> —Shireen Soliman

In this chapter we explore the digital classroom as an opportunity to collaborate and communicate outside a defined meeting time and place. This structure enables students to move through the course experience at a pace aligned with how they learn, providing instructors and students more time for reflection and synthesis. This open and flexible structure offers students a more sustained and ongoing experience, giving them agency in the course that benefits them as learners.

REDEFINING TIME AND SPACE

In previous chapters, we've examined concepts that are situated with the teacher and the student, which give rise to good online teaching and learning such as engagement and inquiry. In this chapter, we are exploring not the actions of the teacher and the student, but the spaces and timeframes within which they practice and study. Within this context, we take a closer look at the potential online provides for the design of multiple learning spaces and extending time for students to engage and ask questions. The models most educators have developed for teaching and learning are designed with the constraints of a physical classroom in mind. Things that teachers may have only thought about as secondary to the learning experience, such as walls, desks, and whiteboards, with school schedules and travel times to and from school, are reassessed in light of online teaching and learning. The digital learning environment invites educators to adapt how they understand the structures of the classroom by providing a more malleable appreciation of time and space with its own opportunities and constraints.

Teaching online can be more adaptable than on-ground teaching, as interactions are not limited by time constraints or physical space. Synchronous interactions occur even with students and instructors in different time zones and locations. Different platforms have distinct structures and spaces: a Zoom meeting can be one room or multiple breakout rooms, discussion forums can be linear or threaded, and a Google document can be a published text or act as a resource for asynchronous or synchronous collaboration. Asynchronous interactions can happen before or after synchronous meetings, expanding on the time in which learning can happen; they can also replace synchronous meetings altogether. Students and teachers can participate and connect at times that are beneficial to their needs. The space of the physical classroom is replaced by the more malleable and multidimensional space of the Internet.

In this chapter, we share how practitioners take advantage of the different possibilities that time and space offer. Some practitioners approached the time and space of online teaching and learning with the intention of reproducing or making up for the lack of physical interaction or a standard time format, finding powerful ways to continue the effective on-ground practices they cherish. Others used the potential of online time and space to try something new or to address challenges that the traditional structures of time and space posed for them. Most practitioners developed purposeful ways of using the opportunities these new ways to flex time and space provide to serve their needs and the needs of their students. They shared examples of how online teaching gives them opportunities to increase engagement, maximize classroom presence, improve their efforts toward equity, deepen inquiry, and strengthen the learning community.

The possibilities of online time and space offer instructors the opportunity to reframe how they interact with students. Online teaching makes time more malleable, as it is not limited by when we all meet in the same space. Some of the practitioners we interviewed invited us to question the value of the structures that were historically designed for the limitations of time and space with on-ground schooling and to consider how they should organize their teaching when those limitations are not relevant anymore. Jesse Stommel explained, "We are used to being required to have butts in seats for specific amounts of time, at a particular schedule, and we don't think about how much of that is really necessary." Dave Cormier also questioned the meaning of the work hour in courses and how we partition and measure course time. He questioned the idea of the student work hour now that we don't need to physically come together to hear somebody talk. The online environment, he said, forces us to ask "what the flow of a student-centered classroom should really look like."

Making use of time and space in ways that benefit our teaching and learning involves a creative change in focus, centering our goals on translating our teaching to a new environment. It requires practice and consideration of our practices in light of different constraints. We found that this is an ongoing process

> **QUOTABLES**
>
> How can I use the online teaching space to allow for depth rather than breadth? —Soyoung Park

and requires finding what works best for ourselves and the students we are teaching.

USING SYNCHRONOUS AND ASYNCHRONOUS TIME AS CLASS TIME

Time between online class meetings can be used for more than readings and homework assignments. Kristen Sosulski finds that instructors new to teaching online sometimes forget about the asynchronous engagement time as an important part of the course. The teacher has the power to redefine how time is structured in the online course. "Online, the time that we have together is precious." Sosulski emphasized that we need to think about what happens before, during, and after different engagement points, stitching together a robust learning experience, an experience that is less about limitations and more about accommodation, providing opportunities for conversations that are parallel to events impacting the students and the world in which they live.

Experienced teachers may change the structure of their courses to take advantage of asynchronous interactions. They find ways to make time and space adapt to the flow of the course community instead of adapting the course because of restrictions on time and space. They use these interactions to deepen conversations, help students prepare for class engagement, and encourage more reflective responses to what is being shared and discussed. Soyoung Park explained how online teaching helps her to use time more flexibly and effectively, transcending the boundaries of time and space that come with on-ground teaching. With the potential of asynchronous classrooms to capture and maintain student interaction beyond the institutional time structures, Park uses

> **COUNTERPOINTS**
>
> Something I've struggled with in online teaching is my presence. For whatever reason, when we meet synchronously, if I share my screen and talk to the students about some information, I feel like I lose them. But I create videos in Canvas, highlighting key points that I hope are thought-provoking, and throughout the video they pause and comment on the prompts I give them. In this video format, they're way more engaged and present. I find that I hear some voices that I don't normally hear in synchronous sessions. Also, when we're in a synchronous session it's hard for me to see everyone at the same time and I can't get a sense of all their ideas, but with their video comments, I can really see everyone's thinking and get a sense of what their big ideas are. And it helps me plan for my synchronous session. I feel I get a better sense of my students when I'm able to read all of their voices in this way. —Soyoung Park

the time between meetings to extend student discourse, letting conversation flow according to the needs of the class and not cutting it short because time is up. She noted, "It just feels like the conversation doesn't have to end when the synchronous discussion ends, and if we dug into something really deep, then that's okay because we're going to keep exploring it throughout the week. You have a chance to look at the asynchronous work and engage with what is being shared again and again." Online students arrive to class better prepared because of the possibility of interacting asynchronously before meetings. Park said, "I've noticed in the conversations in the breakout rooms that students will reference back to the asynchronous posts and things they saw other people writing in there in the conversation, so the asynchronous activity and the work in the class feel very connected."

In asynchronous interactions, the exchanges are recorded, making them a lasting document of student thought and reflection that goes beyond a scheduled class meeting time, making it available for reconsideration and revision. Kristine Rodriguez Kerr said, "There is something really nice about the lasting record of student engagement that you can track as a faculty member in an online course that you can't do in a face-to-face course. I'm not going to remember what a student said in Week 2 of a face-to-face course by the end, but in the online course, I have a record of it." Margaret Terry Orr also finds it very useful to have a record of the interactions that happened throughout the course. Orr describes how she uses digital whiteboards, such as Google Jamboard, as a record of student interaction. The whiteboard is used to collect students' thoughts over time and they can go back and look at what they were thinking throughout the learning experience. At the beginning of her doctoral dissertation seminar, Orr's students discuss theories for facilitating change and collaboratively construct a template that draws on those theories, creating a record of their collaboration. Toward the end of the course, as students work on their research problem, Orr tells her students to go back to their template and use it to facilitate change around their particular research problem. She reminds them that during their time together they have created their own study resource, out of their own thought processes, that they can use to support their academic work.

Asynchronous class work, such as discussion board exchanges, has the added value of giving students and teachers time to think and reflect on what is being discussed. They can enter the class conversation at a time when they are ready to learn and they can take their time, reading what others have said, crafting their response over time and after thoughtful consideration. Online discussions trade spontaneity for the ability to thoughtfully respond to the discourse, which allows time for collecting one's thoughts and for other voices to play out in the conversation. Asynchronous time also allows the teacher to think further about how the students are responding and students can keep thinking about responses and reflections and continue to question what ideas and challenges have developed in the class discourse.

The time to think can push teachers and students to go further with their ideas and assumptions. It also gives the teacher the opportunity to intervene less and wait for the students. Rodriguez Kerr gives an example of this in her teaching, "I don't have to respond right away. If I think someone's posted something that's angry, I don't necessarily need to address it at that moment. I can wait and see what happens, how other people take it. I can also respond in a back-channel way that isn't in front of the whole class. I can wait to see if other questions come up about it."

Jessica Blum-DeStefano also highlights how asynchronous interactions are valuable to instructors by giving them the time to consider the situation. She asked,

> What does this tell me about this student? How can I pay attention to my own reaction? What is that telling me about my thinking, my meaning-making, and what would be a productive, thoughtful, meaningful way to respond, to interject in this conversation to honor where that student is, but to also speak toward larger value systems? Specifically, when we're talking about race, identity, those kinds of conversations, I love having a minute to be purposeful in my answer.

On the other hand, online interactions may feel more formal and permanent because they leave a record. What is said in the on-ground classroom lives in the moment and is more ephemeral than what is written on a discussion board. Blum-De Stefano explained, "There's a heavier lift to put the right words, being intentional, it takes more energy to think because it is going to live in the forums forever. And I imagine it's the same for students." She added that this permanence of thought can be challenging as it may make it harder for students, and teachers, to change their thinking. "I love when I can capture a student's immediate idea and we talk about it and that idea evolves into something else, but something about having it live on a board—that's their idea for the whole week. So that part, I think, is hard." The potentials and limitations of synchronous and asynchronous time and space mean that teachers need to be more aware of which aspects of the course are best suited for real-time, on-camera interactions and which aspects are

For Your Consideration

Often, leadership will say, "Faculty don't need all these bells and whistles." They'll use that in a pejorative sense, when a faculty may actually be saying, "No, it's not a bell and whistle. I use this tool and I use it to effectively engage my students." What we really haven't looked at is how colleges select and buy technologies for online learning, especially the LMS. What do they look for? Is what they think are bells and whistles actually tools for supporting effective teaching?
—Shawna Bu Shell

best for interactions done at one's own pace and in one's own environment. The malleability of online teaching and learning requires more intentional course design.

Many practitioners describe how teaching online has improved how they write assignment instructions, making them more explicit and clearer. In the absence of that physical presence, teachers providing a review of expectations may address in advance questions that students asked about the assignment in previous terms, they may use images, audio, or video to explain or demonstrate tasks. Online students benefit from these personal and engaging instructions when they are looking to understand assignments. Langdon Graves described how she uses multimedia in her instructions. "I mostly do step-by-step photo instructions and a voiceover. I record myself explaining what I'm doing in each one. So the students hear me, and there is warmth in my voice and then I'll create a video if there's something I really want them to see in action, like what a scumbling technique looks like versus a wet brush." Graves uses VoiceThread, a multimedia tool with an interactive discussion space, which helps her to share instructions and respond to students' questions. She also appreciates the alerts VoiceThread provides to notify everyone when someone posts or responds to a discussion. VoiceThread makes her asynchronous class interactive because it helps her keep track of everyone's progress as they work at their own pace.

Graves also blends synchronous and asynchronous work in interesting ways. She adds options and gives students more autonomy. She explained,

> One hour I'm online and around if they need me and it's like drop-in hours. And then there are three hours of asynchronous work. But I'm available to them all the time. With them, it could be so much more playful. I have a set curriculum and things I want to do that day. We're going to take 45 minutes for group work. I put them in breakout rooms, they can play music. And when I visit, I jump around to different rooms, I want to see their progress. I want to see what they're working on, I want to hear; I'm like a fly on the wall a little bit, but I'm there to help and chat with them as well.

The online classroom is a layered classroom and both synchronous and asynchronous modalities provide numerous opportunities for the teacher to connect to the students and for the students to connect with one another. Teacher and student interaction is not dictated by the clock on the wall. Instead, learning can happen fluidly throughout the week, with students connecting with members of the classroom community and the Internet community. And time doesn't always mean moving forward online. It may also mean going back and reflecting or taking side roads to get to a new understanding. Students can be pushed out into the digital classroom and told to come back on their own terms after they have reflected on or engaged with something that they have found to be purposeful and meaningful.

PRIORITIZING RESPONSIVENESS AND FEEDBACK

Continuous communication and flexibility of time make online courses suited to experimentation and trying things out with students. We can make timely adjustments, connect immediately to our students, and modify prompts and guidelines at any time that are responsive to students. "Teaching is fluid," Genevieve Lowry said.

> I think the online space allows for that fluidity. I think teaching is something that has to be; when students need something I can be responsive to that. Every group of students who come in is different. The cohort has its own personality and then each group of students has its own personality, and then each student has their own personality. I have some cohorts who want more synchronous sessions. I have some students who say, "Okay, you don't need to meet with me. I'm good with what's been shared." I have some students who need more hands-on, more one-on-one, who are having different things happening in their lives that require me to provide a level of flexibility where I say, "Okay, let's think about how you can still be engaged but not feel so overwhelmed by the structures that are in place." Being able to be flexible with online structures is key because the point isn't that a student gets something in by the deadline. The point is to understand the course concepts. If you need a little more time to understand a concept, then I want to give that to you as long as the learning happens within the timeliness of the semester. I have students who are in internships and they're overwhelmed and they're exhausted. So for me to publish a module on a Saturday instead of a Sunday and to allow them the extra room to post on a Saturday the following week rather than feeling like I need to receive it by 9 o'clock on Friday is okay.

The practices that Lowry describes highlight the potential the online teacher has to transition among the various needs of the learning community. The expansion of time throughout the course week brings with it the expansion of the teacher's bandwidth to work with students' needs. Students can be responded to and supported at the distinct moments in time that they need support and Lowry can assess those needs and adjust the flow of the course throughout the week, changing how she connects with the students, whether it's asynchronous or synchronous or one-on-one or as a whole. Even better, she can choose more than one way of connecting to meet various needs. From this experience, she can also disrupt the class experience as she developed it, making changes to resources, content, activities, and assignments based on how the students are responding and replying within the fluid timeframe she has constructed. Online teaching and learning is less confined by imposed time and space constraints but that does not mean there should not be limits. The limits or guidelines need to be set by the teacher with the course design and explicit information on the syllabus.

The malleability of time allows us to make these decisions based on what we value. We found that the teachers we interviewed prioritize activities that help their students learn, such as using time for hearing different voices and creating community, or allowing time for reflection. The themes of the five previous chapters of this book highlight those values.

Responsiveness is important to the design of digital spaces. In web design, responsiveness is the art of ensuring that sites on the Internet are accessible to all users. Making the online classroom responsive requires a commitment to ensuring that the teaching and learning taking place responds to the various learning needs of the students who make up the community. The expansion of time and space through increased teacher–student communication, and the fluidity of the course structures to adapt to student inquiry and engagement, provide the potential for teachers to increase and target feedback based on the learning that is happening over time.

Tips

The blog is not a space where I post discussion prompts, but my own reflection on the readings for the week. And then there's just a Slack space where they can go in and they can just comment like crazy and do whatever they want to in that space. I don't provide discussion prompts. I don't tell them, This is what you should talk about this week. I provide the readings and then I provide them with a space to talk. And none of that is graded space. So they actually feel freer to just talk about whatever comes up for them. —Sean Michael Morris

FLEXIBLE SPACES AND MULTIPLE VOICES IN THE CLASSROOM

The online classroom space is very flexible; it can be a really large meeting hall or a small cozy room. You can create multiple spaces with breakout rooms, and have parallel public or private communications using chat. Graves noted that space can be created immediately online. "Online we have breakout rooms. When I'm in the classroom on campus, I can't say I have these six extra classrooms available, but when you're in the breakout room, you actually get some privacy." Grouping and regrouping students for group work is easier and less time-consuming online. Synchronous breakout rooms enable teachers to switch groups and randomize which students work together without being too disruptive. In the on-ground classroom, students tend to congregate with like-minded thinkers in every class and need prodding to establish new groups, which can take away from class time as students manage the logistics of switching. Online spaces make it easier to change groups throughout the semester, and teachers can establish whether groups are intentional or random, based on the needs of the learning community.

The online space also encourages teachers to strive for class discussions that are less hierarchical and more equitable. Amy Khoshbin pointed out,

> When we teach in the classroom environment, there's a power hierarchy in the way that the teacher stands and the students sit. Even if you have everyone sitting in a circle, the way the teacher may be projecting something on the wall, and how everyone's looking and engaging with it, can contribute to that power dynamic. What was amazing about the way that being online affected my classroom is that in the non-hierarchical space of Zoom, everyone is an equal measure talking head. This interaction space—coupled with the chat function—broke down the barriers to enter into the conversation for folks who might not have been as comfortable otherwise. We were able to have 4-hour-long conversations where everyone was a cohost. And so a student would be sharing their screen, impromptu presenting to the class while sharing information they wanted to bring into the conversation.

The dismantling of the enclosed classroom space does offer teachers the freedom to consider less hierarchical structures for the classroom community. While teachers may ask the students to access resources and interact through the LMS, the LMS is not the classroom. It is just one of many components that support the experience of the community learning online. With the removal of the physical space, the teacher may use other structures than the metaphor of the room for teaching. For example, we can use the metaphor of community instead of that of a class, and create a community together instead of imposing the structure of the traditional classroom, removing the inherent hierarchy of the tangible space. We can give the students the opportunity to be more vocal in how the goals and objectives of the course are experienced and expand the role of the teacher to more than just the center of the learning experience, as in a traditional classroom. Teachers can find new ways to manage and inspire the learning community besides claiming sole authority as dispenser of knowledge and holder of power.

Classmates logging on from separate physical spaces may feel disconnected from one another; instructors can design the online space to create interesting and meaningful connections by acknowledging the physical spaces the students are in. In his online course, Jonathan Iris-Wilbanks replicates a connection-building activity he does on-ground in which students bring artifacts to school to share about themselves. Obviously, he could not do the activity exactly the same way online. However, new possibilities opened up as the students were at home and had their personal world around them. He asked his students to open their spaces to the class, sharing where they were at that moment in time. He found that the personal insights gained through this exercise were powerful for establishing connections among the students.

Some online instructors also use the student's real space to do activities that require some physical action and then have the students share that experience with the class. Rodriguez Kerr asks students to use information from their own personal spaces to engage in class conversation.

> I like to have students go into their physical locations, do something, and then bring it back to the course in some way. When I'm teaching a research course, it's usually "Go somewhere nearby for 10 minutes, sit, observe the location, take notes, come back to the course and post your notes." And I'll usually ask students to not post any context, to just post their notes, their photographs, or a thing that they did, but not to explain it in the discussion forum because I want classmates to ask questions. And so that gets the conversation going [. . .] and really rich conversations come up about where students are. And so that is a way for the course not to just be me giving information and them taking it up, but they are going out into their locations and bringing those back into our course site. And I think that's an affordance of an online space.

Quotables

I'm interested in those faculty who had to go online, whether they liked it or not, and they're still there. In some cases, the pandemic removed the resistance to online and these faculty thought, "Oh, if I'm going to practice online, I'd still want to be the instructor I want to be. How do I do this well?" And then there were others who phoned it in and hated every minute of it. I feel like it's a lost opportunity if we don't consider all the things that enhance our practice by being online. Even if you prefer to teach on ground, there are things that make you look at your practice closely, examine it, and learn from this examination. I wonder what is happening to those folks who are saying, "No, I hated it and I don't ever want to do it again." When they go back to the on-ground classroom, is there an awareness that there were things they could do online that they can't do on ground? Perhaps they might then consider embracing a hybrid approach. —Rena Palloff

It may feel contradictory to argue that studying online opens more opportunities to engage in physical space, but students participating from their home or neighborhood can step out of the "classroom" and into their own community to explore, retrieve, and share the things they are experiencing daily. This may allow a working adult to test hypotheses about a strategy taught in class in the workplace in real time, or a student to interview a local expert or revered community leader and bring insights back to the class.

The online classroom gives the student the ability to step back and forth between the learning community and lived community for the enhancement of both spaces.

The space in which teachers and students interact is a mediated space. This mediation brings opportunities for teachers to play with the space as a media space. Iris-Wilbanks uses the mediated space of the screen as an opportunity to modify the traditional expectations of the physical classroom. In his practice as a child life professional, Iris-Wilbanks works with children in the hospital and uses puppets to communicate with them. One of his passions is using the in-hospital television network to deliver large-scale therapeutic experiences to his patients. In his graduate teaching, he found that synchronous video has similarities to that of a televised experience in its creative potential. He uses the mediated experience of the synchronous class to create an interactive experience using puppets. As he described,

> I'll bring in the puppet that I use in the hospital and it will be the puppet attending class. And I use this time as a way to practice talking about death and dying with a child. I'm not on the screen, Frederick (the puppet) will be the one on the screen. And it breaks the role of the professor and the teaching space because Frederick is very childlike and the students know that when Frederick is in class, it is a chance for them to talk to him about death so that they just get the experience of using the words and the language and trying some things out. And the puppet plays the role of a child. It's one of the affordances I really like for breaking down this more formalized space—that the puppet can be a little silly about the awkwardness of Zoom, like group silences and mute buttons not turned off. And he'll say, "Maybe nobody told you, you can press this button and your microphone will turn on. And it's me, it's Frederick." And then more people will turn their microphone on and try talking to the puppet. And they will have deep conversations. And wherever they go in the conversation, I'll go with them. And I'll try to give them what a child would give them. If they ask something too close to the wound, Frederick will change the subject or get mad or just kind of shut down. And it actually works better on Zoom because otherwise, I'd have to hide under a desk. I really have fun with this and folks who are a little less participatory come out of the woodwork a little bit and say "Hi, Frederick, I'm over here."

Merle Keitel, who teaches counseling, also found that the online space worked better than the physical space to create an environment of professional practice. She explained,

> The breakout rooms actually enabled the students to shut their cameras off, leaving just the counselor and the client on screen. And so they didn't feel observed. Even though they knew they were being observed, it wasn't the same intensity as people being over them. And I think that frees them in some ways and

helps them get to a point of greater confidence and less anxiety. So that also enabled them to feel safe in a group of their peers and really get to know one another very well, which I think also increased the safety they felt in the larger class when we had lecture discussions.

TIPS

You have to be able to think about what it is that you're trying to accomplish and do under a particular set of circumstances and what are the affordances of the resources and tools that we have available. And that's what happens in world-building. I think it can't help but influence what you do in your pedagogy and what you do in instructional practices because you don't see limits, you see possibilities. —Detra Price-Dennis

The mediated space can be more easily structured to fit a variety of needs. With even small changes, teachers can reframe how they interact with students. Cali Morrison shares an example of how renaming and redefining communication structures make a big difference in how those structures shape interactions with students. Morrison renamed Office Hours as Student Hours. She leaves the video conference room open and students pop in when they have the opportunity. She found that this small change increased the number of students who come to talk to her.

With online spaces teachers and students are a click away from any other place. There is no need for travel time or change in physical location. There is also no need for the transitional moment of entering the room, settling into chairs, opening notebooks, etc. However, students still need to transition to classwork, they need to disconnect from other activities and be fully present in class. Troy Pinkney finds that her online students need the emulation of transition to help them be present in the online classroom. She builds in transitions that prepare students for learning.

> Whenever I do synchronous sessions with my students, we do some type of meditation. Sometimes it is a breathing meditation, sometimes it's a relaxation meditation, sometimes it's drawing or coloring or writing poetry, something to bring people into the space. I also play music as students come into the space and I do it at the end because it feels like a nice way to close the space. I think that to enter into this space, business-as-usual, "This is what we're going to do," does not allow students to enter and switch gears from whatever they were doing prior to coming into this space. So it's creating space in the online environment to have a space to settle prior to going into whatever it is we're going to be doing.

Pinkney finds ways to intentionally create the benefits of transition and informal classroom interactions. "I think it's really important to be able to give people that space, that transition time. It doesn't just happen in the online environment, you need to do it. There needs to be a time for students to transition."

THE INTERNET AS COMMUNITY SPACE

As online courses take place on the Internet, teachers and students have access to the multitude of voices and resources that live on the World Wide Web. B. Stephen Carpenter II, who has taught art and art education courses for more than 25 years, found that teaching online makes it easier for him to connect his students to resources and to find examples to share spontaneously as he needs them. He said,

> If I were in a ceramics class, for example, where I want to talk through some ideas, like form or another concept, I might refer the students to other artwork, noting, "Here are some images of an artist's work." I might not have it prepared in a lecture; if we're in a critique, I wouldn't have lecture notes for a critique, I would, in the moment think "Oh, you need to look at these artists X, Y, Z." It's easy to have Google open, and pull something up and pop it on the screen whether it's on the Internet or in my reserve of images or readings. I wouldn't have all of those things necessarily with me in the studio or the classroom, but I have them here on my computer.

Since online courses exist in digital time and space there is greater potential for the teachers and students to connect to people, places, and ideas outside of the class community. Chris Friend explained,

> Going into the outside world and bringing it back into the class is so easy in an online class because it all happens in the same space. We can find things that are online and bring them into a place that's already online. If we have a conversation that is in a discussion thread or if I mentioned something in class, and then I wander off and I'm living my life and I'm reading the news or I'm finding articles online or I am having a conversation with other people and find that it refers directly to what we were talking about in class, I can then go back to that asynchronous conversation and follow up and say "Hey, this just happened there; I just noticed this, and it reminded me of this conversation we were having before." And we can do that in an open platform, where students can access it at any time and they're able to say "Oh, I was just out here in the world, and I noticed this thing that's relevant." These things don't have to happen all at the same time, and that allows us to make connections.

The experiences that Carpenter and Friend describe nicely highlight the layered space that is the online classroom. These layers include the numerous points online that make up the formal online environment. This traditionally starts with the LMS, but also includes synchronous tools, various applications for social connecting and learning support, and sundry education-focused technologies. Then there are the spaces the community reside in physically, whether that be the more specific spaces, such as their homes, classrooms, or offices, or the more social spaces of the world in which they reside physically, such as the neighborhoods around them or the families that support them. And then there is the space that connects the teacher and the students and mediates the learning experience, the Internet itself. With this space there is a cornucopia of access to information and people, and while it can be overwhelming to travel out into this abundance, with the right guidance and frame of mind, you can locate and connect to resources that enliven and energize inquiry and understanding.

Holding class in a digital space creates opportunities for people in different locations to participate in the class discourse, which supports teachers in bringing in experts and experienced professionals, including different voices as sources of knowledge and enhancing the learning experience. As Iris-Wilbanks noted,

> I think one thing the online teaching has afforded me is that I can bring my colleagues in a lot easier. My colleagues who are running the Child Life Disaster Relief System out of St. Louis can join us on a Zoom. I bring in the professionals from the field; I get the nurses and the spiritual care providers, the social workers, the occupational therapists, and the doctors, I really try to bring them into the class. You can't learn this from one White guy. It's not good for your education. You need these perspectives and different people and backgrounds and professional abilities.

Teaching in an online format has afforded Iris-Wilbanks the opportunity to bring professionals into the learning space and students into the professional space. "Our medical info class this semester is taught by the Chief Resident of Pediatrics at Oakland. And traditionally the students would go to Oakland and

Counterpoints

There tend to be two approaches educators take with technology. The first is that pedagogy should drive everything, that we should make our pedagogical decisions first and then choose our technology. The other is that there's a shiny new piece of technology, "Look at what it can do. Let's use that." And we try to fit our teaching around what this amazing thing does. However, I think when you look at how learning happens with technologies, it's a much more entangled exchange across what people desire to do pedagogically and what technologies are designed to do. —Jeremy Knox shadow a doctor. But he suggested, 'Why don't we just bring the students virtually into case consultations with the whole team of residents?'"

Connecting the course to the news and media and finding more relatable examples supports teachers in demonstrating the application of theoretical concepts in ways that make them more accessible for students. Graves links information from current happenings and social media to get students interested in participating in ongoing conversations about a course topic. As Graves shared, an example of this is how she turned the story that went viral about people seeing the colors of a dress differently into a color theory lesson. She brings the world in to get students interested, making class topics matter in her students' lives.

Using social media as part of their courses provides students the opportunity to go beyond the walls of the classroom and to engage with the world outside. Having her students leave the classroom gives Christina Katopodis the ability to create more engaging and authentic assignments that have real audiences with people in the field. As she explained,

> We were reading a book by a scholar whose work I really admire and a student was tweeting about it and the author of that book tweeted back at her. And she was so excited that the author responded to her and engaged with her blog post about this topic. And she was just kind of floored and amazed. And I could see how joyous and how meaningful that was to her, that it wasn't just validation from me. It was validation from the author of the book that she was talking about, which was huge for her.

For Your Consideration

One of our ceramics instructors was looking to teach materiality at a distance. He asked students to look at vessel forms and understand the volumetric nature of them. Then, in their dorm room or wherever they were, they had to find objects and stack them or tape them together to make forms, and then shoot them with a digital camera. The students were adjusting the lighting as they were creating these images. They were creating essentially vessel sculptures, because they were trying to convey the concept of volume. Clay isn't just about the medium here, but clay is the medium for the object they are referencing. —B. Stephen Carpenter II

Susie Rolander also found that Twitter allowed her class to connect with experts outside the classroom. "Twitter feels really powerful, because if we think about bringing the outside world into the learning space, we're creating a Twitter feed that has experts on it, who you can learn from and connect with. You have access to a much larger world. It's such a big expanse, so that's why I think Twitter is pretty powerful for teaching and learning." Rolander also cherishes her use of Twitter because it allows her students to stay connected to her after the course is over, transcending the official timeframe of the course. She said, "Just recently I had a student reach out on Twitter asking me about books. I had him in class 5 years ago and he moved away, and yet we still connect on Twitter, so it feels like there is this breaking down of walls that I just love and it's changed how I teach."

Being in the same online space can motivate the relationships and ideas of a course to transcend the time in which the course lives. The work of Khoshbin's students went beyond her scheduled class time.

> My students ended up creating their own organization called Brooklyn Engaged, which they're wanting to hand off to the next social practice class, while also continuing to participate in it. And I think a lot of that had to do with the fact that we don't have to be in the same physical space, because some of these students are moving back to the West Coast and still want to be involved in the project. That wouldn't have been possible without digital learning.

The online classroom can be transformed into different spaces, making it possible for the classroom to include a multiplicity of environments. Jeremy Knox shared that in his program faculty think of the different ways they want students to engage and the different environments and tools they can use to fit those purposes.

> If we need to do a more focused discussion on some readings, then the discussion forum is fine. But if we want to do more a quick-fire building of ideas, maybe we take that out onto Twitter, where we wouldn't need such deep reflection and where students don't mind being public and a bit more informal. So digital spaces can be conducive to different kinds of group activities. We're always trying to make the learning environment as diverse as possible. We have always been critical of the idea that there is one space that can do everything.

The idea that online space and time can be described as authentic may sound surprising to some, especially those who may use the idea of what is real as a way to distinguish between the physical and digital classroom. However, in coming to understand the spaces and time frames of the online learning experience, it is a misnomer to define them as "virtual," if that means they are somehow unreal. While the digital aspects of online learning may lend themselves to the creation of spaces that appear gamelike or immersive, our interest in time and space has more to do with the possibilities of extending the learning community and experience beyond scheduled meetings in a room on campus. There is nothing virtual about students connecting with real-world experts or extending successful class-based projects to the 16th week of class and beyond. In this light, online learning becomes less about an emulation of the traditional classroom and more of an advancement of all that has come before. It is this understanding of time and space in the online classroom that should help to guide practice. These concepts can guide us to consider not what we can do within the standard time frame of the traditional classroom, but what we can do to create experiences that extend beyond those limitations to help students understand the real impact they may have on themselves and the world in which they live. How can the flexibility and access of the online space develop learners ready to lead and guide in the fields they have studied?

Ask Yourself

What time or space constraints shape your course?
As you design your online course, how do you focus on space beyond the classroom?
How do you take advantage of asynchronous time and multilayered spaces in your online classroom?

CHAPTER 7

Conclusions

Shifting Your Mindset and Sifting Through Your Residue

> We are what we repeatedly do. Excellence, then, is not an act but a habit.
>
> —Will Durant, *The Story of Philosophy*

In this chapter we provide signposts and pathways for new and experienced educators to grow and deepen their practice online. We consider how the different concepts described in Chapters 1 through 6 are connected to an evolving pedagogy, and conclude by examining lingering issues and encouraging readers to expand the possibilities for teaching and learning online.

CHAPTER HIGHLIGHTS FROM OUR EVOLVING PEDAGOGY

We start our conclusion with a summary of the topics that were presented in each chapter. Some of these ideas are well-known among educators but we hope that these stories offer some new ways of understanding.

Engagement

We began by exploring the concept of engagement as central to the online classroom. We describe what engagement looks like as an active contribution to the class inquiry by distinguishing it from participation and connecting it to a view of the classroom as a community. In an engaged classroom, everyone shapes the discourse. The teacher does not sit at the center of the classroom but is one more member of the learning community. Teachers do not have predetermined answers. Instead, they embrace the uncertainty of co-constructing the course with the students they teach. Engagement originates from the experiences that develop when getting to know each other as learners in the community, so the aim of the activities is to get the students engaged in conversation.

The online classroom and its technologies can be used to inspire engaged interaction. The online classroom can include different forms of collaboration, documenting engagement and the learning process through time, making the learning experience visible and available for reflection. We offered specific activities that encourage the students to share their identities and interests, making authentic connections possible.

Students come to our classes with different experiences and need opportunities to learn how to engage authentically. Teachers show the students how their engagement positively impacts the course community, and this encourages them to engage further. We also explored the ways in which curriculum design offers the students opportunities to act as contributors to the course content and co-constructors of the curriculum.

We closed the chapter with ideas on how we can assess engagement. The data most valuable to the teacher is the overall view of engagement within the community as this data helps the teacher learn and make adjustments to improve course engagement overall.

Inquiry

Chapter 2 defined inquiry as the experience of seeking understanding through authentic questioning that promotes knowledge ownership and engages all learners in a collective intellectual endeavor. An authentic approach to inquiry requires a commitment to believing in the capacity of students to ask questions and pursue answers, and that of teachers to let go of the need to provide definitive answers. Together, teachers and students can embrace the uncertainty required for learning to happen.

We looked at how inquiry shapes course design with different examples, such as how overloading a course with content hinders students' ability to ask questions. In their online courses, teachers create more opportunities to ask students their thoughts and their questions by using polls and surveys, low-stakes prompts and reflective journals, which open up the classroom to more voices and ideas. Knowing our students is essential to inquiry as learning is connected to students' identities. The design of the online classroom can be structured to make students feel that they are in a good place to ask questions. Some teachers encourage their students to question the learning environment itself, and commit themselves to designing the online classroom as a flexible and fluid environment for student learning.

The chapter highlights how teachers are immersed in inquiry themselves. Teachers describe how they take a learner's stance to inquire about their own online teaching. They take an inquiry approach to their curriculum and encourage their students to contribute to the content. We are better teachers when we ask more questions, are reflective, and are learners ourselves.

Equity

In Chapter 3 we explored how online teaching addresses equitable access for all students. We look at equity as access to the technologies used for teaching and learning, addressing what it means to let others into your home and the privilege of having a private space. Different practitioners shared the importance of offering guidelines and giving choices to students for bringing themselves to the classroom and inviting them to lean in with their whole selves.

We explored how the online classroom can be less hierarchical than the traditional classroom by providing multiple pathways so students know their authentic voices are welcome and are willing to engage. Practitioners shared how their online classrooms are more open to opportunities for when and how students communicate, making class discussion more inclusive. Others focused on equity by helping students develop an awareness of the impact online technologies have on their learning. And others emphasized the importance of the ongoing work of all in the learning community, acknowledging and understanding diversity, equity, and inclusion to ensure we are serving all students.

Presence

Chapter 4 explored how students and teachers are present in the online course. Teachers shared the need for students to go beyond performance and create an authentic presence in class. All agreed that knowing and understanding our students and creating relationships are essential to inviting authentic presence. Teacher presence is essential for student engagement. Teachers who make their investment in student engagement explicit support the students in understanding presence.

We discussed the idea that teacher presence does not depend on synchronous interactions and can be embodied in the design of the course. Some teachers found that using video is another way to be present. Some teachers found that supporting presence requires them to deemphasize their own voice and invite multiple ways for students to share theirs. Teacher presence is visible in online courses as students see that teachers are following the flow of their development and the course itself changes with them.

Communities

Chapter 5 addressed how intentionally building a community is essential to online teaching and learning. Building community is not dependent on physical space or physical interaction. The teachers we interviewed described community building in the online space as authentic, dynamic, and emotional, and they focused on the interactions they wanted to nurture. In deconstructing and reconstructing their teaching online, practitioners discovered new possibilities for showing student work collectively, highlighting its permanence in time, and sharing it beyond the classroom community. In teaching online, they found ways to learn about the communities in which the students live and work, and to know them as the multifaceted human beings they are. By taking advantage of the possibilities for interaction online (synchronous or asynchronous, whole group, small group, or one-on-one, in text, audio, video, or combined) teachers have more opportunities to bring people together to create inclusive communities, which they find is easier to accomplish online than on ground.

This chapter also explored the idea that learning communities online can go beyond the course community, inviting external practitioners who can share their perspectives or adjacent communities who can provide authentic audiences for student work. The educators we interviewed highlighted how they benefitted from being a part of other communities themselves, designing courses collaboratively, and supporting each other by sharing their experiences for advancing online teaching and learning.

Time and Space

In Chapter 6 we explored how time and space are more malleable and multidimensional in the online classroom than in the physical classroom. We saw how teachers developed purposeful ways of molding time and space to their benefit and the benefit of their students. We discovered the need to question some assumptions regarding how we measure learning time and the amount of work assigned, and how to consider what guides those decisions.

Teachers use asynchronous time to extend interaction time. They take advantage of written and recorded interactions to engage in revision and reflection, as this allows for a return to ideas that develop as the course evolves. Asynchronous interactions give all learners time to reflect before they engage, allowing for more voices and ideas to enter into the conversation. Some teachers found that the online classroom is better suited for the fluidity of teaching. Since online courses exist in digital time and space, there is a greater potential for teachers and students to connect to people, places, and ideas outside of the class community. The malleability of time and space also means that the relationships forged during the course can continue after the course has ended because time and space are not what holds the class together. It's the relationships themselves.

In offering this summary, we hope that we have inspired you to think about how you can transform your online teaching practice. The practitioners we interviewed stated again and again that their practice was built over time, with multiple iterations of action and reflection. We now share how one of us embarked on this process of researching her own teaching practice.

A WAY FORWARD FOR DEVELOPING YOUR ONLINE PRACTICE

The power of our narrative is in the shared stories and experiences of our fellow online educators. Retaining what we treasure most about our practice while opening our hearts and minds to new and different ways of thinking about our work empowers us. What we offer now is a way forward for understanding our practice deeply in order to continue making our teaching even stronger and more substantive. Our question—How will examining our practice closely influence and enhance our online teaching?—will support us in discovering pathways for growing and innovating our practice.

One way to support growth and innovation is by engaging in action research, which is a powerful pathway in effecting change. Action research is a way for us to look closely at a specific aspect of our online practice in order to gain a deeper understanding of it. The methods of action research support inquiry and reflection, using our work as data. And through action research, we invite others to join us in building relationships that promote collaboration.

While there are many structures and approaches for crafting action research, an ideal approach is one that is not predetermined or planned out without any space for movement. The approach is more organic rather than technical—based on what the researcher wants to pursue and how the researcher wants to pursue the question. A thoughtfully crafted question that is personally compelling, some literature that has influenced our thinking, a mindful and practical methodology, and a way to analyze the data collected, will lead to discoveries that, when shared, will influence others.

In her dissertation, *Exploring Action Research as an Enduring Experience of Professional Development for Teachers,* Robin Hummel (2017) explained that action research requires embracing a learner's stance as we consider our work through the lens of an action research question. We accept that research is an essential element in developing one's practice and that valid research emerges from reflections on our work that is often already in progress. As discussed in an earlier chapter, Appreciative Inquiry (Carr-Stewart & Walker, 2003; Cooperrider & Whitney, 2005; Hammond, 2013) focuses on the positive core of our work and what most inspires us. Taking what we are already doing, what we already cherish about our work; asking probing questions that will support us in examining our practice with a keen and focused eye; and taking action on those probing questions, will move us forward in our online teaching practice.

In *Leadership and the New Science: Discovering Order in a Chaotic World* (2006), Margaret Wheatley led us to consider how the effect of Newton's "new science" had a parallel in our own field. Hummel (2017) wrote,

> The Newtonian paradigm that emphasizes a mechanical and hierarchical model of [learning and teaching] is still alive and well in spite of the fact that the new sciences (chaos theory, systems theory, and quantum theory, for example) no longer view the world in such a linear way. In these new sciences, our world is much messier, more surprising, paradoxical, and interconnected than we could ever have imagined. (p. 18)

Adult development theorists suggest that when we are in over our heads (Kegan, 1994) in dealing with pressing, complex problems, the only solution is to grow—to develop our level of mental complexity. Margaret Wheatley (2006) gives us some hints about what that might look like. In the service of values that include compassion, justice, and human development, we need to think in ways that are more dynamic and less static, appreciate and accept apparent paradoxes, look at our work as connected to our intellectual growth rather than disconnected components, seek distributive rather than hierarchical power, and focus on synergy rather than scarcity. In a mindful action research process, teachers have the support to develop a level of mental complexity within a nurturing learning community.

As you consider immersing yourself in an action research question as a way to move your online practice forward, it is wise to find a collaborative community of action researchers—those interested in pursuing their own questions while supporting yours. "Action research is not a solitary pursuit" (Hummel, 2017, p. 110). Part of the power of action research comes from discussing the challenges and learning one encounters throughout the process of action research and sharing findings with a broader audience. One of the most satisfying aspects of pursuing action research is the ownership of our own inquiry. Fischer (2001) pointed out that as we discuss our work with our colleagues we find our own voices emerge more clearly, and our ideas and research questions evolve. And we find great sustenance in the meanings we discover in telling our stories of teaching online.

We have been pursuing our own action research around engagement in online environments for some time. Early in her online teaching, Robin coauthored a chapter about creating and supporting engagement. That piece was focused on discussion forums and engagement that transcended participation. Fast forward to now, and she finds herself still struggling with figuring out ways to structure reading assignments that inspire engagement.

Robin's commitment to a learner's stance through action research compelled her to ask, How can I structure reading assignments to create authentic, purposeful, and consistent engagement? By asking this question, she learned important lessons regarding how her expectations might be obstacles for students to truly engage. She assumed that her students, freed from prescriptive directions (e.g., post once by a certain date and respond twice to classmates, or vice versa), would respond to one another in the forums just as they do in her physical classroom. The truth is, she confessed, that even in her physical classroom she really had no way of knowing for sure whether students had even done the reading before coming to class, nor did she monitor all of their conversations in on-ground groups to see if they did. She would listen as she walked around the classroom, but wasn't actually assessing the substantiveness of the exchanges, nor did she necessarily know what the students were learning or what questions they had unless they offered them during the wrap-up. Going online certainly diminished those issues—she found there was much more accountability when students needed to respond to a prompt—and people had plenty of time and space to bring up confusions and questions and additional thoughts without worrying that the class was over. But again, it didn't necessarily lead to a less perfunctory exchange, even when she came up with a great prompt or removed all of the restraints of when to respond and how often. She just knew she wanted to transcend the superficial ping-pong-like game of back-and-forth exchanges and think about how to make it more of a cocktail party, where you go in and out of certain conversations, stick around and engage in the ones that entice you, and move on from the ones that don't.

Right now, she is experimenting with Hypothesis, a tool which supports a synthesis of reading and responding. Instead of students reading a piece and coming back to the group to exchange thinking in a discussion forum, students annotate and comment simultaneously. What were once two distinct actions is now one. The issue she's grappling with now is defining what she really means by engagement. Does everyone have to annotate something from the text? Is it considered engagement if, as they are reading, they are simply responding to someone else's comments? Isn't that what happens sometimes in an authentic exchange? Not everyone has to contribute an original idea or quote directly from the text in order to keep a conversation moving. And as far as checking for understanding, in responding to someone else's comment, doesn't that give the instructor information on what the reader understands? These are some of the ideas with which she continues to grapple.

Recently, she's come around a bit and adjusted her laissez-faire approach to how she wants students to engage. Some students need scaffolding. So in a recent assignment, she asked students to read the piece and find three to five salient points they want to make or questions they want to ask within a certain time period, and then go back in and respond to posts that provoke them in some way. So far, the scaffolding has given better access to those proverbial late posters and has leveled the playing field for those who need more time to think about what they want to contribute.

For Robin, pursuing questions for action research exemplifies the idea that teaching and learning are synonymous. "Teachers who are committed to the art and scholarship of teaching understand that their teaching practice fuels their learning, and their learning fuels the scholarship and art of teaching. What a teacher does in the classroom is as much about one's own learning as it is about student learning" (Hummel, 2017, p. 7).

LINGERING ISSUES AND THE POSSIBILITIES OF TEACHING AND LEARNING ONLINE

Good teaching and learning does not depend on the space in which the teacher stands or sits. It depends on the teaching itself. We doubt that any of the teachers who have generously shared their practices in this book would describe themselves, first and foremost, as *online* educators. We assume that, instead, they would simply declare themselves to be educators. And as educators are wont to do, they took an invitation to teach online as an opportunity to better understand their practice. With everything that we have shared in the previous chapters, we would ask that if you take nothing else with you, take this: Online teaching is akin to any other teaching experience in that to be successful you must be willing to adapt your practices to meet the needs of your learners. You must be flexible and open to change. This receptiveness to teaching online as an invitation to innovate your practices is important, because otherwise it is easy to become mired in discussions that present online teaching as less than teaching. Such arguments run counter to the idea we are sure of, which is that good teaching is independent of where the teaching takes place. Furthermore, teaching that invites the student to present themselves as a whole person and to go out into the world to strengthen the learning in the classroom affirms the relevance of online as a space with the potential for deepening student experience and thought.

In developing your online practice, keeping in mind the potential of online teaching as transformative will be helpful to you if you encounter situations that make teaching online feel less than inspiring. There are an abundance of demotivating potholes on the road toward the development of robust and authentic online experiences. Take as an example the structured learning management system (LMS) templates your institution uses. They may be so methodical that you may feel as though you are designing a static digital textbook instead of an exhilarating learning experience. Or consider the in-house academic staff there to support your online efforts. While they may be well-intentioned, they may also be overly committed to what they deem "best practices based on research" for course design and the use of prebuilt course shells that stymie or stunt exciting opportunities to explore the potential that online has to shape practice. The examples teachers shared with us are meant to help you avoid the types of traps that institutions may unknowingly set in the quest for quality. We acknowledge that standards for online course development are useful for teachers new to online teaching and learning, but this book does not speak to that stage of online teaching. The practices shared are for teachers who reach that moment when they have heard all that has been said by their institution and they are now ready to transform and innovate their digital classrooms.

In each chapter, we have shared practices that not only inform your online teaching, but also inch you toward the potential of online education. We would argue that any teacher stepping into the online classroom should take the opportunity to reassess their approach to teaching and learning. We readily confess that even while we considered ourselves progressive and transformative educators, when we first entered into our online classrooms we were felled by various traps. We took the long way to discovering the need to adopt a different way of thinking about our practice and how to make our digital classrooms authentic. We found out that teaching online often brings with it the need to accept that we are teachers learning all over again and that we have a rare opportunity to learn from every new exciting discovery and challenging misstep. Every educator remembers what it is like being a first-time teacher, and it is hard to go back to that mindset; and yet, seeing your classroom with the eyes of a new teacher, where there are no limitations, only discoveries, is a good way to start thinking about how to teach online. Moving from How do I *translate* what I do in my online classroom? to How do I *transform* what I do in my online classroom? is a big step toward innovating your practice and, quite possibly, the overall online experience at the institution where you teach.

Before we close, we would like to remind you that your digital classroom is a portal to a more expansive universe for teaching and learning. The opportunities that online teaching and learning offers are more than the features of the learning management system your institution uses. As you grow your online practice you can also grow the features of your online classroom. You can go from designing lessons for online learning to adopting a world-building approach and creating interactive activities to inspire question-driven learning communities. You can go from designing syllabi outlining structured modules to developing flexible spaces where the curriculum shifts in response to student curiosity and interest. You can go from gathering students into small online groups to encouraging them to seek out networks external to the classroom yet accessible via the Internet. Whatever else you take away from what you have read, remember that there is only one good response to the question, What does online learning look like? Just like for any other teaching experience, the one answer is that there is no one answer for what good teaching and learning looks like online.

While we hope these final thoughts inspire you to imagine the possibilities of how to best design an online classroom that is adaptable to student inquiry, vocal because of student equity, and authentic due to student engagement, we also accept that what we have shared may be daunting at best and impossible at worst, due to internal policies and expectations established by the institution where you teach. As any teacher might attest, being an innovative teacher is challenging. Yet anyone who teaches understands that being an innovative teacher always means testing and assessing your practice. We would add that successful innovation comes with an openness to letting ideas grow with the students and encouraging them to take the reins of the learning experience to captivate their quest for knowledge. The role of the teacher then becomes monitoring the seeds they have planted, watching them grow and blossom, and, in the end, reflecting on how to expand on the successes that have happened so that the next group of learners can benefit from the innovations that previous students have helped to shepherd.

Let us conclude with one more thought on how you can come to online teaching and learning wearing the hat of a transformative and innovative online educator. It is best when you arrive at the doorway of your online classroom that you leave behind any preconceived notions of what your teaching will look like online. Instead, when you reach that moment when you begin designing your online course, before you meet with academic leadership or instructional designers, before you tour the learning management system, before you copy your previous course content to your new course environment, and before you do anything that anyone might present to you as the standard first step for teaching online, stop and reflect on your practice. What is it that you do as a teacher that makes learning successful? We encourage you to assess your practices based on the following broad points that encapsulate the areas we have discussed throughout this book to guide practice toward transformative and innovative online teaching and learning.

Ask yourself: Do the practices that I use to support student learning:

- Encourage discussions and interactions that are engaged and engaging? Do they go beyond prompts and assignment directions?
- Provide opportunities for me to present myself authentically, and do they also provide opportunities for students to be authentic in the classroom?
- Offer moments to acknowledge and adjust my approaches to teaching and learning based on the questions and inquiries students are asking and sharing?
- Help to form learning communities where voices are inclusive and equitable on a micro level (from inside the classroom) and a macro level (that surrounds the classroom)?
- Support linkages to online networks and denizens that give my students access to knowledge that strengthens their understanding of the course knowledge and of what it means to be an inquisitive learner?
- Transcend traditional constraints rather than remain mired in the physical classroom, and present themselves as good practices no matter where and how they are experienced?

If some of these points are familiar to you and you see them in your practice, we invite you to use them to push your practice forward. And if you are thinking that your practice does not reflect these points, do not fret.

Remember, just by considering these aspects you are taking a giant step, and if, after reading what we have presented, you consider adjusting and strengthening your practices to create online experiences that are engaged, present, inquisitive, equitable, communal, and flexible, then you are on the right path. If you need inspiration or ideas for where to go next, we suggest you go back through the book and look at some of the examples shared and see if there are any kernels of inspiration to try in your online classroom. And always remind yourself that good online teaching is, in the end, good teaching.

References

Brookfield, S. D. (2000). Transformative learning as ideology critique. In J. Mezirow & Associates (Eds.), *Learning as transformation* (pp. 125–148). Jossey-Bass.

Brown, J. S. (2002). Learning in the digital age. In M. Devlin, R. Larson, & J. Meyerson (Eds.), *The Internet & the University: 2001 Forum* (pp. 65–91). Forum for the Future of Higher Education and EDUCAUSE. http://www.johnseelybrown.com/learning_in_digital_age-aspen.pdf

Carr-Stewart, S., & Walker, K. (2003). Learning leadership through appreciative inquiry. *Management in Education, 17*(2), 9–14. doi:10.1177/08920206030170020301

Cherches, T. (2020). *VisuaLeadership: Leveraging the power of visual thinking in leadership and in Life.* Post Hill Press.

Cochran-Smith, M., & Lytle, S. L. (2001). Beyond certainty: Taking an inquiry stance on practice. In A. Lieberman & L. Miller (Eds.), *Teachers caught in the action: Professional development that matters* (pp. 45–58). Teachers College Press.

Cooperrider, D. L., & Whitney, D. (2005). *Appreciative inquiry: A positive revolution in change.* Berrett-Koehler.

Dewey, J. (1938). *Experience and education.* Kappa Delta Pi.

Fischer, J. C. (2001). Action research rationale and planning: Developing a framework for teacher inquiry. In G. Burnaford, J. Fischer, & D. Hobson (Eds.), *Teachers doing research: The power of action through inquiry* (2nd ed., pp. 29–48). Lawrence Erlbaum Associates.

Freire, P. (1993). *Pedagogy of the oppressed: Newly revised 20th Anniversary Edition.* Continuum.

Garrison, D. R., Anderson, T., & Archer, W. (1999). Critical inquiry in a text-based environment: Computer conferencing in higher education. *The Internet and Higher Education,* 2(2–3), 87–105. http://dx.doi.org/10.1016/S1096-7516(00)00016-6

Garrison, D. R., Anderson, T., & Archer, W. (2007). Researching the community of inquiry framework: Review, issues, and future directions. *The Internet and Higher Education, 10*(3), 157–172. https://doi.org/10.1016/j.iheduc.2007.04.001

Giroux, H. (2011). *On Critical Pedagogy.* Bloomsbury.

Hammond, S. A. (2013). *The thin book of appreciative inquiry* (3rd ed.). Thin Book.

Hummel, R. (2017). *Exploring action research as an enduring experience of professional development for teachers* [Dissertation, Fielding Graduate University]. ProQuest.

Kegan, R. (1994). *In over our heads: The mental demands of modern life.* Harvard University Press.

Kohn, A. (2015). *Progressive education: Why it's hard to beat, but also hard to find.* Bank Street College of Education. https://educate.bankstreet.edu/progressive/2

Shor, I., & Freire, P. (1987). *A pedagogy for liberation: Dialogues on transforming education.* Bergin & Garvey.

Stommel, J., Friend, C., & Morris, S. M. (Eds.) (2020). *Critical digital pedagogy: A collection.* Hybrid Pedagogy.

Veblen, T. (1908). The evolution of the scientific point of view. *University of California Chronicle, 10*(4), 395–416.

Wheatley, M. J. (2006). *Leadership and the new science: Discovering order in a chaotic world* (3rd ed.). Berrett-Koehler.

Index

About the Authors

Steven Goss, EdD, has been a leader in online teaching and learning for over 20 years. He has led successful online programs and initiatives at Teachers College, Columbia University, Bank Street College of Education, and New York University, including the establishment of The Center for Faculty Innovations in Teaching and Learning at NYU Tandon School of Engineering. He has taught diverse student audiences, including K–12, undergraduate, and graduate. His courses are closely related to his academic interests, including instructional design, teacher practice, and experiential learning. He has received awards from The Association for the Advancement of Education in Computing (AACE) and Online Learning Consortium (OLC) for his research on learner-centered online education. Dr. Goss received his EdD in instructional technology and media from Teachers College, Columbia University, and holds an MA from New York University and a BS from Pennsylvania State University in Art Education.

Robin E. Hummel, EdD, is codirector of Online Teaching and Learning at Bank Street Graduate School of Education, where she supports faculty in the development of progressive pedagogy online. Dr. Hummel is also the director of the Leadership in Mathematics Education program. As Bank Street faculty, she serves as an advisor to graduate students and teaches mathematics, mathematics pedagogy, and action research. She received her EdD in leadership for educational change at Fielding Graduate University in Santa Barbara, CA, and her dissertation focused on action research as professional development for teachers and leaders in schools. She has presented at the Online Learning Consortium and the American Educational Research Association. Prior to her career in higher education, she taught 5th grade through high school in public schools for over 25 years in southern New Jersey.

Laura Zadoff, EdM, is codirector of Online Teaching and Learning at Bank Street Graduate School of Education, where she supports faculty in teaching with technology and is engaged in the development of new online programs. Prior to Bank Street College, she worked as an online coach for teachers for Wide World, an online teacher professional development program at

Harvard Graduate School of Education, and as an instructional designer of online courses for the Educational Portal of the Organization of American States. During her studies at Teachers College, she was a research fellow at Columbia University's Center for Teaching and Learning. Laura received her EdM in instructional technology and media from Teachers College, Columbia University, and her Licenciatura in communication and education from Universidad de Buenos Aires, in Argentina.